MW00364681

48 Healthy No-Bake Protein Bar Recipes
To Satisfy Your Sweet Tooth!

Jessica Stier

Copyright © 2018 Jessica Stier

All rights reserved. No part of this book may be reproduced or transmitted, in any form or by any means, without consent from the author.

This book is intended as a reference only, not as a medical manual. It is not intended as a substitute for any professional medical advice, diagnosis or treatment that you may have been prescribed by your doctor. Every human being is incredibly unique, so what may "work" for one person may not necessarily "work" for you (and vice versa). Always seek the advice of a physician and registered dietitian where appropriate.

Nutrition labels provided in this book were accurate at the time it went to press.

Milky Way®, Snickers® and Twix® are registered trademarks of Mars, Inc. Reese's®, Almond Joy®, Mounds®, Pay Day® and Take 5® are registered trademarks of The Hershey Company. Nutella® is a registered trademark of Ferro, SpA. Cherry Ripe® is a registered trademark of Cadbury, Ltd. All trademarks remain property of their respective holders, and are used only to directly describe the products referenced in this book. Any mention of specific companies in this book does not imply endorsement by the author.

Book design by Amanda Parker of Marathon Designs.

ISBN-13: 978-1-7320476-0-0

Third Edition

Raspberry Almond Protein Bars, pg. 15

CONNECT WITH ME

f .... www.facebook.com/DessertsWithBenefits
www.facebook.com/DIYProteinBarsCookbook

🐦 .... @DWBenefits
@DIYProteinBars

📌 .... www.pinterest.com/WithBenefits

📷 .... @DessertsWithBenefits

🌐 .... www.DessertsWithBenefits.com

✉ .... Jessica@DessertsWithBenefits.com

Don't forget to tag what you make on social media with the hashtags
#DIYProteinBars and **#DIYProteinBarsCookbook**. I'd love to see your recreations!

DEDICATION

I wrote this cookbook for all the Desserts with Benefits® fans who have asked me to write one throughout the years that I've been blogging. With the heaping amount of support I've received along the way, this publishing experience can only be described as extraordinary.

With every comment, *I am thankful.*

With every email, *I am touched.*

With every shout-out, *I am over the moon.*

With every testimonial, *I am eternally grateful.*

With all the encouragement, *my nerves poof into thin air.*

The friendly online community that I am in inspires me more than words can ever describe.

So THANK YOU!

Thank you, my lovely blog readers. You are inspiring, uplifting, and kindhearted souls.

TABLE OF CONTENTS

White Chocolate Macadamia Protein Balls, pg. 37

ABOUT THE AUTHOR

Jessica Stier is the author, photographer, and recipe developer behind the *DIY Protein Bars Cookbook*, which was inspired by her healthy dessert recipe blog, Desserts with Benefits® (www.DessertsWithBenefits.com). She is a healthy dessert expert with an interest and a strong scholarly background in the fields of Nutrition and Dietetics (thanks, university!), but before college she was the complete opposite. I guess we should start from the beginning, shall we?

I was born and raised in a quiet, homey neighborhood in Calgary, Alberta, Canada. Like most kids, I ate whatever I pleased. I plowed my way through boxes of candy bars, jumbo-sized bags of chocolate goodies, and enough candy to fill dozens of Halloween trick-or-treat pumpkin baskets (i.e., enough sugar to make the most seasoned sugar fiend sick with a stomachache and candy hangover).

When my family uprooted to the United States, so did my sugar addiction. All the way to age eighteen, I ate poorly (understatement of the year?) and didn't exercise. I ate chocolate bars for breakfast (yes, I'm serious), a bag of chips, "fruit" snacks, and a carton of sugary chocolate milk for lunch (are you getting a sugar rush just by reading this?), and something else nutritionally deficient for dinner, like nachos or instant noodles. I brought so much candy to school that I was known as "Hershey Girl," "Sourpatch Girl," and even just plain old, "girl with candy."

After every meal, I felt gross and uncomfortable with a foggy brain, but I kept on eating the unhealthy foods I had always eaten. A diet like that seemed normal. My family ate like that, the kids at school ate like that, it tasted good… so, what's the problem?

When I turned sixteen and got my first job at a pretzel joint in the local shopping mall, I gained a little bit of weight. And by "a little" I mean "a lot." Like, twelve pounds in three months. This was a huge shock to me. I never gained weight like that before despite my inadequate diet and sedentary lifestyle. I may have been on the thin side my entire life, but I was always "skinny-fat." A lot of jiggle on bones with no muscle whatsoever.

My solution? Oh, just buy those 100-calorie snack packs and (attempt to) stop eating a bajillion pretzels dunked in butter every time they began to look dry. Yeah, that didn't fly. The excess salt, the dangerous trans fats, the highly refined sugar, the artificial sweeteners… it just made me want more. A lot more. And I paid the price for it – I was an emotional roller coaster with crazy cravings, either trapped in a steady state of lethargy or stuck in an unstoppable yo-yoing between sugar rush and sugar crash.

I just wanted to be better… healthier.

With perfect timing, I graduated high school and was about to enter university – a brand new stage in life where I decided to start over. Completely. I chose to major in Nutritional Sciences, and this was one of the best decisions

I have ever made. I learned everything under the sun about food, nutrition, and the human body. I finally came to terms with my own body, the reasons why I ate the way I did, and how I should be eating. Now, just a few years later, I have finally found the solution to achieving consistent energy levels, and I am satiated for a long period of time (no more of those "I-must-eat-that-entire-tray-of-brownies-ASAP" feelings). I have boosted my metabolism, put on lean muscle (~15 pounds), and have lost some fat (~10 pounds).

I ~~lived~~ for chocolate. I live for chocolate.

Don't get me wrong, I still indulge. I have (and will always have) a serious passion for sweets! I have just learned how to make those sweets secretly healthy.

Enter, Desserts with Benefits®

My blog was born late at night on April 20th, 2011 as a serious procrastination technique to avoid studying for finals. I didn't post a recipe, but rather, a list of desserts that were on my "Baking Wishlist," along with dishes that I've made but had turned out unsuccessful. Healthy baking is a difficult thing to do! I don't use sugar (white granulated sugar, brown sugar, high fructose corn syrup, etc.), artificial sweeteners (aspartame, sucralose, etc.), white flour (all-purpose flour, cake flour, pastry flour, bread flour, bleached flours, etc.), or unhealthy fats (hydrogenated shortening, margarine, genetically modified oils). I mean, anything can be made to taste good using all the wrong ingredients, but is it what your body wants? I don't want my desserts to give off the same repercussions that typical unhealthy desserts do (aka, bloating, headache, stomachache, nausea).

When I started blogging, I hoped to show people that healthy ingredients can indeed make a delicious cake, muffin, pastry, cookie, and so on.

I am happy to say that, with the hundreds of testimonials I've received, with the loyal Desserts with Benefits® fans who comment regularly, and with the thousands upon thousands of people around the world who have tried (and loved!) my recipes…

I have met that goal.

ABOUT THE COOKBOOK

The *DIY Protein Bars Cookbook* is a collection of 48 healthy no-bake protein bar recipes to satisfy your sweet tooth! And there are options for everyone. The recipes are (or can be easily made) gluten-free, dairy-free, soy-free and vegan... but you'd never know it. One bite of any protein bar in this cookbook and you'll be screaming, "OH-MY-GOSH-this-is-so-freakin'-good-how-can-this-be-good-for-me?!?"

runs around in circles with joy

(Yes, that will happen.)

These protein bars are so tasty and addicting you'll never buy store-bought again! Every protein bar recipe contains complete proteins (they contain all the essential amino acids). Protein is essential for muscle growth, repair and maintenance, and it is also necessary for maintaining blood pressure, fluid balance, pH balance and electrolyte levels within the body. The amount of protein you need is unique to you, but for the average person, it is recommended that you consume .8-2 grams of protein per kg of body weight. Personally, though, I think this puts too much of an emphasis on getting enough protein rather than eating a balanced diet, so I like to go by this:

10-35% of calorie intake from **PROTEIN**

20-35% of calorie intake from **FAT**

45-65% of calorie intake from **CARBS**

I like to have my protein bar recipes fall somewhere within these ranges, but we don't need to go all "Anal Retentive Chef" here (thanks, Saturday Night Live)! These recommended percentages have a pretty wide range, and depending on what stage you are in your life – whether you're an athlete or a vegan, whether you're a growing teen or a pregnant woman, etc. – you can modify these numbers to suit your needs. I always recommend meeting with a registered dietitian if you need some help (they don't bite, I swear)!

Each recipe in this cookbook includes a nutrition label so you can see how many calories, grams of fat, carbohydrates, protein and fiber are in each serving. No matter what, though, there are options for everyone's nutritional preferences: sugar-free, refined sugar-free, cholesterol-free, low-calorie, low-sodium, high fiber and high protein. These recipes might be "free" of some stuff, but they sure aren't free of flavor!

Oh, and don't you worry, the fun doesn't stop there. Every recipe in this cookbook is all natural – no artificial sweeteners, no synthetic food dyes, no artificial food flavorings, no hydrogenated oils and no preservatives whatsoever. That list right there is unheard of when it comes to store-bought protein bars.

Let's all make the same, scratch that, better versions of store-bought protein bars right at home.

These protein bars are perfect for both pro and novice athletes. After an intense workout, they're the best reward for sweating like an animal, dealing with your exhausted muscles, and trying to control those damn uncontrollable jelly legs.

But that's not all. Protein bars aren't only for the workoutaholics.

Do you have a sweet tooth?

Did you just raise your hand? Then these protein bars are for you too. They taste like candy bars (seriously, just check out the **Candy Bar Protein Bar section on pg. 83-102**) but without all the excess calories, fat and sugar. These recipes are a total godsend for the health-conscious dessert lovers out there (aka, YOU). If you occasionally crave (and when I say "occasionally," I really mean "incessantly") a big hunk of – for lack of a better word – sugar in a wrapper, make a batch of protein bars instead and you'll be happy as can be… no guilt involved.

In The Buff Protein Bars, pg. 90

Let's Race Protein Bars, pg. 91

PANTRY STAPLES

THE PROTEIN POWDERS

Brown rice protein powder is often the main dry ingredient and cannot be omitted. It might be possible to substitute it with other vegan protein powders (such as hemp, pea or soy), but every brand is different so I can't vouch for any other powders. Whey, casein, and egg white protein powder will not work in place of the brown rice protein. You will get a sticky, gooey mess on your hands. Delicious sticky gooeyness, but difficult to make and impossible to slice.

ORGANIC BROWN RICE PROTEIN POWDER
Nearly all of the recipes in this cookbook use brown rice protein powder. It is hypoallergenic, sugar-free, gluten-free, dairy-free, nut-free, vegan and non-GMO. I use SunWarrior® Classic Protein in both Vanilla and Chocolate. I attempted these recipes with 2 cheaper brands but paid for it in the end – they made the grittiest, most unpleasant bars!

ORGANIC GRASS-FED WHEY PROTEIN POWDER
One recipe in this cookbook uses whey protein powder because it is widely available and it is perfect for people who aren't vegan or allergic to dairy. I buy whatever brand is cheapest, but also organic, grass-fed, non-GMO, and sugar-free.

NUT AND SEED BUTTERS

Nut and seed butters are used in every single recipe in this cookbook! They are full of healthy fats, fiber, and essential nutrients. While some are high in protein, they are incomplete proteins (lack essential amino acids) so they need to be paired with something else to create a complete protein, such as oats, beans, etc. Always use natural nut/seed butters without added sugar, salt and oil – the ingredient list should contain only one ingredient: the nut/seed itself! Slightly runny nut/seed butters are ideal for these recipes. If you can, buy organic. If you want to make nut/seed butters at home, see **Getting Started on pg. xiv.** If you are allergic to nuts, simply replace the nut butters with seed butters.

NUT BUTTERS

Raw and Roasted Almond Butter
Roasted Cashew Butter
Raw Coconut Butter
Roasted Hazelnut Butter
Roasted Macadamia Butter
Natural Peanut Butter
Roasted Pecan Butter
Roasted Walnut Butter

SEED BUTTERS

Pumpkin Seed Butter
Sunflower Seed Butter
Tahini (Sesame Seed Butter)
Hemp Seed Butter

THE FLOURS

ALMOND FLOUR
Almond flour is ground up unblanched almonds. I use Now Foods® almond flour.

OAT FLOUR
Oat flour is simply ground up oats. I use Bob's Red Mill® certified gluten-free oat flour because it's whole grain, finely ground, easy to use, has a great flavor and is safe for people with celiac disease. Oat flour is difficult to replace in these protein bars recipes because it absorbs moisture and binds the mixture, allowing the protein bars to firm up nicely in the fridge and not fall apart when you slice and hold them.

COCONUT FLOUR
Coconut flour is ground up dried coconut. I use Nutiva® because it's gluten-free, organic, non-GMO and inexpensive (from Costco!). It has a mild sweet, coconut flavor. Coconut flour is difficult to replace because it provides a specific texture and absorbs so much liquid.

PEANUT FLOUR
Peanut flour is a defatted flour made from ground peanuts. I use Protein Plus® roasted all-natural peanut flour, which is high-protein, reduced-fat and gluten-free. Peanut flour is difficult to replace because it absorbs moisture, binds the mixture, provides extra peanut flavor and a punch of protein. ¼ cup of peanut flour has 110 calories, 4g fat, 8g carbs, 4g fiber and 16g protein. ¼ cup of peanuts has 170 calories, 14g fat, 5g carbs, 2g fiber and 7g protein.

NON-DAIRY MILKS

I have nothing against dairy milk as long as it's organic, I just prefer to use non-dairy milk because it has a longer shelf-life and won't spoil if the bars happen to drop to room temperature.

UNSWEETENED VANILLA ALMOND MILK
I use Silk® unsweetened vanilla almond milk (30 calories per cup). You can find it in the refrigerated section. I find that it has the best taste and creamiest texture, and I like how it's non-GMO.

UNSWEETENED VANILLA COCONUT MILK
I'm not a huge fan of coconut milk as I prefer the flavor of almond milk, although I must admit it's suuuper creamy. Hence, I don't have a favorite brand. I just borrowed (okay, stole) a few cartons from my sister's place to make these recipes... I have a feeling she won't be reading this (she's the kind of person who skips right to the recipe without reading the instructions) so please don't tell... shhhh!

Unsweetened Vanilla Soy, Cashew, Hemp, and Rice Milk should work just fine too! If using soymilk, always buy organic and non-GMO. Never conventional... ever.

CHOCOLATE

Chocolate... CHOCOLATE... CHOOOOCCCOLLAAATTEEE!! Yes. You will need chocolate to make some (ehem, a lot) of the recipes. This is what you'll need:

Milk Chocolate with
Salted Almonds
(I use Theo®)

Milk Chocolate
(I use Green & Black's®)

White Chocolate
(I use Green & Black's®)

Bittersweet Chocolate
(I use Guittard® or Green & Black's® 70% cacao)

FLAVORINGS

Always use natural flavors. If available, use organic too.

EXTRACTS AND SUCH
- Almond Extract (I use Simply Organic®)
- Banana Flavor (I use Bakto Flavors®)
- Blueberry Flavor (I use Bakto Flavors®)
- Butter Flavor (I use LorAnn Oils®* or Silver Cloud Estates®...I buy whichever is cheapest)
- Butterscotch Flavor (I use Frontier Co-Op®)
- Cherry Flavor (I use Bakto Flavors®)
- Mint Flavor (I use Frontier Co-Op®)
- Raspberry Flavor (I use Bakto Flavors®)
- Strawberry Flavor (I use Bakto Flavors®)
- Vanilla Extract, Pure (I use homemade** but you can use Nielsen Massey® too)
- Vanilla Bean Paste (I use homemade** but you can use Nielsen Massey® too)

*LorAnn Oils® sells a similar flavoring, the Butter Vanilla Bakery Emulsion, which contains hydrogenated oils! Only buy the Butter Emulsion, which is all-natural, trans fat-free, sugar-free, gluten-free and vegan.

** You can make Vanilla Extract and Vanilla Bean Paste at home! Just go to **www.DessertsWithBenefits.com** and in the search bar, type in: "Homemade Vanilla Extract" or "Homemade Vanilla Bean Paste"

SPICES AND OTHER FLAVORS

- Ground Cinnamon
- Ground Nutmeg
- Espresso Powder
- Brewed Espresso (you can use decaf if you want)
- Salt (sometimes I use Pink Himalayan Salt instead)
- Flaked Sea Salt
- Rum (yes, rum)
- Matcha Green Tea Powder (I use DōMatcha®)
- Original Amazing Grass® Green Superfood® Powder

FROSTINGS, COATINGS, TOPPINGS AND BASES

Protein bars are great and all, but they're so much better with some fun little extras. Like a nice chocolate shell. Or maybe even a chocolate Greek yogurt frosting. Oh, and some sprinkles too!

PLAIN, NONFAT GREEK YOGURT
Always buy plain, unsweetened yogurt to avoid the added sugar, food dyes and other additives. Get organic to avoid the added hormones, antibiotics, steroids, etc.

NEUFCHÂTEL CREAM CHEESE
If you can't find Neufchâtel, just use ⅓ Less Fat Cream Cheese (they're basically the same thing).

MASCARPONE CHEESE
I haven't been able to find organic Mascarpone, but I buy mine from Whole Foods Market® because I trust their products more than the typical grocery store products.

COCONUT OIL
Unrefined coconut oil has a strong coconut flavor while refined coconut oil is neutral. Choose whichever kind you want, just make sure it's non-hydrogenated!

ROASTED ALMONDS, PEANUTS, PECANS, PUMPKIN SEEDS, AND HULLED SUNFLOWER SEEDS

CARAMEL SAUCE
I use Date Lady® Organic Coconut Caramel Sauce because it contains no added sugar (it's made from dates)!

You can also make Caramel Sauce at home! Go to **www.DessertsWithBenefits.com** and in the search bar, type in: "Homemade Caramel Sauce"

PSYLLIUM HUSK POWDER
I use Now Foods® psyllium husk powder. Be sure to use the powder and not the whole psyllium husks.

GROUND FLAXSEED MEAL
I use Bob's Red Mill® whole ground flaxseed meal.

NATURAL RAINBOW SPRINKLES
I use India Tree® natural rainbow sprinkles.

You can also make Rainbow Sprinkles at home! Go to **www.DessertsWithBenefits.com** and in the search bar, type in: "Rainbow Sprinkles"

REDUCED FAT UNSWEETENED SHREDDED COCONUT
I use Let's Do…Organic® shredded coconut because it's organic and contains no added sugar.

GRAHAM CRACKERS
When I make protein bars for myself, I use Mi-Del® 100% whole wheat honey grahams. When I make protein bars for anyone with a gluten allergy or with celiac disease, I use S'moreables®. The nutrition facts for recipes containing graham crackers are calculated using Mi-Del® 100% whole wheat honey grahams.

You can also make Graham Crackers at home! Go to www.DessertsWithBenefits.com and in the search bar, type in: "Homemade Graham Crackers"

PRETZEL RODS
I've used quite a few different kinds of pretzel rods and pretzel sticks, including Mary's Gone Crackers® sea salt pretzel sticks (organic, whole grain, and gluten-free), Newman's Own® salted pretzel rods (organic), and grocery store brand pretzel sticks. I think the pretzel rods are best because they stay the crunchiest the longest. The nutrition facts for recipes containing pretzel rods are calculated using Newman's Own® salted pretzel rods.

ALL-NATURAL VANILLA MARSHMALLOWS
I use Dandies® all-natural vegan vanilla marshmallows.

GARBANZO BEANS/CHICKPEAS
I use canned chickpeas because, to be honest, cooking them takes way too long. Use unsalted chickpeas if you can find it!

CRISPY BROWN RICE CEREAL
I use Erewhon® because it's organic, gluten-free and whole-grain.

QUICK-COOKING OATS
I use Bob's Red Mill® certified gluten-free quick-cooking oats.

QUINOA FLAKES
I use Ancient Harvest® quinoa flakes.

NATURAL SWEETENERS

LIQUID STEVIA EXTRACT
Stevia is an all-natural, calorie-free, sugar-free sweetener (derived from the Stevia rebaudiana herb) that does not affect blood glucose levels. It's 300x sweeter than sugar, so it's really easy to use too much, causing the dish you're making to taste bitter. I use SweetLeaf® because it tastes great and it's organic. In this book, I use the following flavors:

- Stevia Clear (Plain)
- Vanilla Crème
- Coconut
- English Toffee

Another brand I sometimes use is NuNaturals®. Always use alcohol-free stevia!

HONEY
I use Nature Nate's® 100% Pure Raw & Unfiltered Honey. It looks similar to the honey you'll find in those bear-shaped bottles but is just slightly thicker and much tastier!

PURE MAPLE SYRUP
Never use the artificial stuff – it's just high-fructose corn syrup blended with artificial flavors, dyes, preservatives, and all that sorta crappy crap crapola! Pure maple syrup is smooth, luxurious and packed with flavor (and nutrients)!

FRUITS AND VEGETABLES
Fruits and vegetables are used in quite a few recipes. They provide natural sweetness (without having to add sugar), along with some fiber, vitamins and minerals. Always seek organic and non-GMO fruits and veggies with no added sugar.

FRESH	**FREEZE-DRIED**
Beets	Freeze-Dried Bananas
Carrots	Freeze-Dried Cherries
Lemons	Freeze-Dried Raspberries
Oranges	Freeze-Dried Strawberries
Baby Spinach	
DRIED	**PREPACKAGED AND CANNED**
Dried Unsweetened Blueberries	Unsweetened Applesauce
Dried Unsweetened Cranberries	Beets (its juice is like nature's food dye!)
Unsweetened Raisins	100% Pure Pumpkin Puree

ESSENTIAL KITCHEN TOOLS

KITCHEN WEIGH SCALE (A MUST, MUST, *MUST!*)
I make every single recipe using a kitchen scale. In my kitchen, a scale is more important than measuring cups. In the recipes, I start off each ingredient by weight, and then in parentheses, the estimated equivalent in volume. Weighing your ingredients is much more accurate than measuring ingredients with measuring cups. 1 cup of Oat Flour will weigh about 120g sifted, or 180g packed...that is a huge difference that will lead to an even bigger difference in taste, texture and appearance. So stick with the scale! I use my Escali® Arti Glass Kitchen Scale.

ELECTRIC STAND MIXER WITH BEATER ATTACHMENT (OR SUPER BUFF BICEPS!)
Nearly every recipe in this cookbook uses an electric stand mixer. It mixes the dough thoroughly, quickly and easily. You can certainly do without the stand mixer and mix everything by hand, but just know that going that route will take 5x as long (and about 10x more patience). I use my KitchenAid® Artisan® Series 5-Quart Tilt-Head Stand Mixer.

SMALL FOOD PROCESSOR
You'll need this to blend certain ingredients (like freeze-dried fruit), and if you make your own oat flour from rolled oats (certified gluten-free if necessary). I just buy my oat flour because it's finely ground, it's easy to use, it has great flavor and it is safe for people with celiac disease. I use my Cuisinart® Mini-Prep® Plus Food Processor.

MIXING BOWLS
Have small-, medium-, and large-sized bowls.

MEASURING SPOONS
Have ⅛ tsp, ¼ tsp, ½ tsp, ¾ tsp, 1 tsp, and 1 tbs.

MEASURING CUPS
Have ¼ cup, ⅓ cup, ½ cup, and 1 cup.

SPOONS, FORKS, AND A SHARP 9-10" KNIFE

2½" OR 2¾" CIRCLE COOKIE CUTTER

ESSENTIAL KITCHEN TOOLS

FINE-MESH SIEVE

WIRE WHISKS AND SILICONE SPATULAS

8X8" AND 9X9" SQUARE BROWNIE PANS

JELLY ROLL PAN WITH A FITTING SILICONE BAKING MAT
I use a 13x18" jelly roll pan and 11⅝"x16½" Silpat®

PASTRY ROLLER
This just makes your life a little easier when you press the protein bar "dough" in the pan.

MICROPLANE AND GRATER
To zest oranges and lemons and to grate carrots.

CAKE PEDESTAL AND CAKE DOME
You'll need this to store protein bars with frostings since you can't wrap those in sandwich baggies.

PLASTIC WRAP AND PLASTIC SANDWICH BAGGIES

PRE-CUT PARCHMENT BAKING SHEETS (12½X16")
I use If You Care® compostable, unbleached, chlorine-free parchment baking paper.

DOUBLE BOILER
You'll need this to melt chocolate… lots and lots of lovely chocolate! I use my Farberware® 2-Quart Covered Double Boiler. It's perfect for all types of chocolate – white chocolate, milk chocolate and dark chocolate!

GETTING STARTED

How Much Will These DIY Protein Bars Cost Me?

Are you ready for a surprise? Seriously, you ready?

Despite the seemingly expensive ingredients used in this cookbook, homemade protein bars are actually LESS expensive than store-bought protein bars. All you need to do is shop around (most often online, from Amazon.com, ThriveMarket.com, and iHerb.com) for the best prices, find some coupons, use a discount code, and then say "KA-CHING!"

Save money and make nut and seed butters at home. Just go to **www.DessertsWithBenefits.com** and in the search bar, type in "Homemade Pecan Butter" – the process of making your own nut/seed butter is the same for all nuts/seeds. Just swap the pecans in the recipe with whatever nut/seed you like!

STORE-BOUGHT PROTEIN BARS:

Quest® Chocolate Brownie Protein Bar

$2.79

Pure Protein® Chocolate Deluxe Protein Bar

$2.99

PowerBar® Chocolate Brownie Protein Bar

$2.99

MET-Rx® Chocolate Fudge Deluxe Protein Bar

$3.19

DIY PROTEIN BARS:

$1.47	Roasted Almond Butter
$0.38	Unsweetened Vanilla Almond Milk
$0.79	Vanilla Crème-Flavored Liquid Stevia Extract
$6.85	Chocolate Brown Rice Protein Powder
$0.59	Oat Flour
$0.13	Unsweetened Natural Cocoa Powder
$0.00	Salt
$1.01	No-Sugar-Added Chocolate Chips

$11.22	(divide by 10 bars)

Only $1.12 per bar!

That means you can save up to $2.07 PER protein bar!

Prices are obtained from the products' websites and/or Amazon.com (prices vary on Amazon.com and are subject to change). The DIY Protein Bar cost is calculated using the Chocolate Protein Bar recipe (pg. 1) and the ingredients from Pantry Staples (pg. v-xi).

HOW TO LINE YOUR BROWNIE PAN

1. Cut your parchment paper into long strips so that it fits nicely inside your pan. The majority of the recipes in this cookbook call for an 8x8" brownie pan, so you'll need to cut the parchment paper into strips slightly thinner than the size of the pan – about 7½" (if you are using the same pre-cut sheets that I use, simply fold the paper in half widthwise and cut about 1" off the creased side).

2. Place the paper inside the pan, leaving the overhang for easy removal later on. Feel free to use mini binder clips on the sides of the pan to keep the paper in place. This makes it easier to spread and flatten the protein dough inside the pan.

HOW TO MAKE PICTURE-PERFECT PROTEIN BARS

Complete steps 1 and 2 on the previous page, then proceed with the following steps:

3. Make the protein bar recipe and scoop the mixture into the pan.

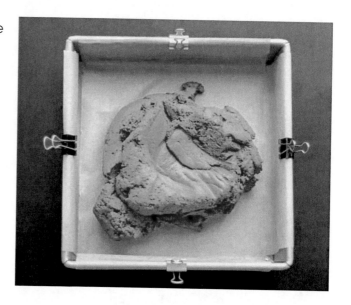

4. Use a silicone spatula to press down on the mixture and spread it to the edges of the pan (pictured on the left). If you want perfectly even protein bars, use a pastry roller after the spatula (pictured on the right).

5. Fold one side of the parchment paper overhang over the flattened protein bars and use your finger to round out the edges. Run your finger along the edge until it's smooth. Do this on all four sides.

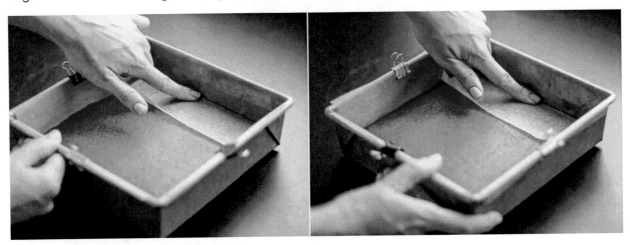

6. Tightly cover the pan with plastic wrap and refrigerate overnight.

7. The next day, remove the protein bars from the pan. Using a sharp 9-10" knife, slice the mixture down the center and rotate. To slice into 10 bars, each protein bar should be around 1½". To slice into 12 bars, slice the mixture down the center again to make a + sign, then slice each square into three long, thin bars.

HOW TO MELT CHOCOLATE AND COAT YOUR PROTEIN BARS

1. Fill the bottom portion of the double boiler with 2-3" of water. Make sure the water doesn't touch the bottom of the double boiler insert! Place the double boiler over medium heat.

2. While the water is heating up, break the chocolate into chunks and place inside the double boiler insert. When the water starts to simmer, reduce the heat to medium-low.

3. Stir occasionally until the chocolate is melted and completely smooth.

4. Place a silicone baking mat on top of a jelly roll pan and line the protein bars on top.

Red Velvet Cake Protein Bars, pg. 40

5. With a large spoon (I use a tablespoon measuring spoon), ladle the chocolate over the protein bars. Try to encase the entire protein bar with chocolate, but it doesn't have to be perfect. An offset spatula makes this super easy!

6. Refrigerate until firm (~1 hour). Individually wrap the protein bars in plastic sandwich baggies and refrigerate to store.

Buuut they're really good right now. So you should totally snack on them. Right now. Ehem...

FINALLY ABOUT TO MAKE A RECIPE? AWESOME! BEFORE YOU DO, READ THIS!

Just as a precaution, always read through the entire recipe once or twice from start to finish before diving in and making some protein bars. Cooking on the fly can lead to some serious kitchen fails (trust me, I've come across every hitch imaginable by cooking without reading the instructions first).

rolls eyes

But I've learned my lesson. I've learned to avoid substituting and omitting ingredients because 99% of the time, it will not work. You will be sad. So sad. The recipes here are tried and true so we can love them the way they are.

Brown rice protein powder is the main dry ingredient and cannot be omitted. It might be possible to substitute it with other vegan protein powders, but every brand is different so I can't vouch for any other types of powders. All I know is that whey protein powder, casein protein powder and egg white protein powder will not replace the brown rice protein powder. I have a tiny bit of experience using unflavored pea protein powder (see the Peanut Butter Protein Bars, pg. 4).

Good news! There are a few ingredient subbing exceptions:

The liquid stevia extract can be replaced with all-natural packeted sweeteners, such as organic stevia, Truvia®, Stevia in the Raw®, etc. Check out the www.DessertsWithBenefits.com FAQ page for a Sweetener Conversion Chart!

You can substitute the almond milk with any other milk -- unsweetened vanilla soy milk, cashew milk, hemp, oat, and rice milk. Regular dairy milk should work just fine too.

Allergic to peanut butter? Maybe all you have on hand is almond butter? No worries! Any nut or seed butter in the recipe can be replaced with another nut or seed butter. Tahini and sunflower seed butter do well to replace peanut butter, and almost any other roasted nut butter works to replace almond butter.

TIME SAVING TIP

Use a kitchen scale! In the Essential Kitchen Tools section on pg. xii, I talk about how I use a kitchen scale to make all of my recipes. A scale helps you measure the ingredients properly so you get the same final product every time you make a recipe. Although, accuracy isn't a scale's only purpose. Using a scale allows you to make accurate nutrition labels (or simply calculate the correct number of calories, fat, carbs, protein, etc.). You also use less cooking materials, from mixing bowls to utensils to measuring cups to measuring spoons. Less dishes to wash? Yes, please. Because that gives us more time to eat.

STORING YOUR PROTEIN BARS

Almost all protein bars keep for ~1 week in the fridge and can be frozen for up to 3-4 months. To freeze, place the protein bars in plastic sandwich baggies, seal tightly, and place in the freezer. If you want to freeze bars that have frosting, like the Birthday Cake Protein Bars (pg. 46), place the bars on a parchment paper-lined tray, freeze uncovered for 4 hours, and then place the frozen solid bars in sandwich baggies. To thaw, simply leave the frozen protein bars in the fridge overnight, or, leave at room temperature for ~3 hours.

If you have any other questions, feel free to email me directly:

JESSICA@DESSERTSWITHBENEFITS.COM

That's it. Let's go make some healthy protein bars!

fist pump

ORIGINAL FLAVORS

CHOCOLATE PROTEIN BARS

MAKES 10 PROTEIN BARS

128g (½ cup) **Roasted Almond Butter (Natural Peanut Butter works great too!)**

1 cup + 2 tablespoons **Unsweetened Vanilla Almond Milk**

1 teaspoon **Vanilla Crème-Flavored Liquid Stevia Extract**

168g (1¼ cups, lightly packed) **Chocolate Brown Rice Protein Powder**

80g (⅔ cup) **Oat Flour**

2 tablespoons **Unsweetened Natural Cocoa Powder**

⅛ teaspoon **Salt**

¼ cup **No-Sugar-Added Chocolate Chips (or Mini Semi-Sweet Chocolate Chips)**

1. Line an 8x8" brownie pan with parchment paper. Set aside.

2. In an electric stand mixer bowl fitted with a beater attachment, add all of the ingredients. Mix on low speed until everything is fully incorporated.

3. Scrape down the sides of the bowl. Mix on medium speed for one last mix. Mixture should be thick and fudgy, like cookie dough.

4. Scoop the mixture into the brownie pan and flatten it out. Tightly cover the pan with plastic wrap and refrigerate overnight.

5. Lift the mixture out of the pan. Slice into 10 bars. Individually wrap the protein bars in plastic sandwich baggies. Store in the refrigerator for up to 1 week or stash them in the freezer.

NUTRITION FACTS	Amount Per Serving		%Daily Value*
	Total Fat 8.5g	Total Carbohydrate 12g	
Serving Size 1 bar	Saturated Fat 1.5g	Dietary Fiber 5g	
Servings Per Recipe 10	Trans Fat 0g	Sugars <1g	
Calories 190	Cholesterol 0mg	Protein 17g	
Calories from Fat 80	Sodium 85mg		
*Percent Daily Value are based on a 2,000 calorie diet.	Vitamin A 0% Vitamin C 0% Calcium 15%		Iron 20%

NUTRITION FACTS

Serving Size 1 bar
Servings Per Recipe 10
Calories 180
  Calories from Fat 70

*Percent Daily Value are based on a 2,000 calorie diet.

Amount Per Serving		%Daily Value*
Total Fat 8g	Total Carbohydrate 7g	
Saturated Fat 1g	Dietary Fiber 4g	
Trans Fat 0g	Sugars 2g	
Cholesterol 0mg	Protein 19g	
Sodium 120mg		
Vitamin A 0% Vitamin C 0% Calcium 6%		Iron 10%

PEANUT BUTTER PROTEIN BARS

MAKES 10 PROTEIN BARS

128g (½ cup) **Natural Peanut Butter**

1 cup + 2 tablespoons **Unsweetened Vanilla Almond Milk**

1 teaspoon **Vanilla Crème-Flavored Liquid Stevia Extract**

168g (1¼ cups, lightly packed) **Vanilla Brown Rice Protein Powder**

90g (¾ cup) **Peanut Flour**

¼ teaspoon **Salt**

1. Line an 8x8" brownie pan with parchment paper. Set aside.

2. In an electric stand mixer bowl fitted with a beater attachment, add all of the ingredients. Mix on low speed until everything is fully incorporated. Feel free to add a handful of chopped, roasted peanuts!

3. Scrape down the sides of the bowl. Mix on medium speed for one last mix. Mixture should be thick and fudgy, like cookie dough.

4. Scoop the mixture into the brownie pan and flatten it out. Tightly cover the pan with plastic wrap and refrigerate overnight.

5. Lift the mixture out of the pan. Slice into 10 bars. Individually wrap the protein bars in plastic sandwich baggies. Store in the refrigerator for up to 1 week or stash them in the freezer.

PEA PROTEIN POWDER VARIATION

128g (½ cup) **Natural Peanut Butter**

1 cup + 2 tablespoons **Unsweetened Vanilla Almond Milk**

1¾ teaspoons **Vanilla Crème-Flavored Liquid Stevia Extract**

1 teaspoon **Pure Vanilla Extract**

130g (1 cup, packed) **Unflavored Pea Protein Powder**

90g (¾ cup) **Peanut Flour**

¼ teaspoon **Salt**

ALMOND BUTTER PROTEIN BARS

MAKES 12 PROTEIN BARS

128g (½ cup) **Roasted Almond Butter**

¾ cup **Unsweetened Vanilla Almond Milk**

1 teaspoon **Vanilla Crème-Flavored Liquid Stevia Extract**

1 teaspoon **Almond Extract**

168g (1¼ cups, lightly packed) **Vanilla Brown Rice Protein Powder**

96g (1 cup) **Almond Flour**

¼ teaspoon **Salt**

1. Line an 8x8" brownie pan with parchment paper. Set aside.

2. In an electric stand mixer bowl fitted with a beater attachment, add all of the ingredients. Mix on low speed until everything is fully incorporated. Feel free to add a handful of chopped, roasted almonds!

3. Scrape down the sides of the bowl. Mix on medium speed for one last mix. Mixture should be thick and fudgy, like cookie dough.

4. Scoop the mixture into the brownie pan and flatten it out. Tightly cover the pan with plastic wrap and refrigerate overnight.

5. Lift the mixture out of the pan. Slice into 12 bars. Individually wrap the protein bars in plastic sandwich baggies. Store in the refrigerator for up to 1 week or stash them in the freezer.

NUTRITION FACTS	Amount Per Serving		%Daily Value*
	Total Fat 9g	Total Carbohydrate 6g	
Serving Size 1 bar	Saturated Fat 1g	Dietary Fiber 3g	
Servings Per Recipe 12	Trans Fat 0g	Sugars <1g	
Calories 160	Cholesterol 0mg	Protein 14g	
Calories from Fat 90	Sodium 95mg		
*Percent Daily Value are based on a 2,000 calorie diet.	Vitamin A 0% Vitamin C 0% Calcium 8%		Iron 10%

COCONUT PROTEIN BARS

MAKES 10 PROTEIN BARS

128g (½ cup) **Raw Coconut Butter, melted**

1 cup + 2 tablespoons **Unsweetened Vanilla Coconut Milk, room temperature**

1 teaspoon **Coconut-Flavored Liquid Stevia Extract**

168g (1¼ cups, lightly packed) **Vanilla Brown Rice Protein Powder**

36g (¼ cup) **Coconut Flour**

⅛ teaspoon **Salt**

1. Line an 8x8" brownie pan with parchment paper. Set aside.

2. In an electric stand mixer bowl fitted with a beater attachment, add all of the ingredients. Mix on low speed until everything is fully incorporated. Feel free to add a handful of unsweetened shredded coconut along with an extra splash of coconut milk!

3. Scrape down the sides of the bowl. Mix on medium speed for one last mix. Mixture should be thick and fudgy, like cookie dough.

4. Scoop the mixture into the brownie pan and flatten it out. Tightly cover the pan with plastic wrap and refrigerate overnight.

5. Lift the mixture out of the pan and let it sit on the counter for 10 minutes to soften. Slice into 10 bars. Individually wrap the protein bars in plastic sandwich baggies. Store in the refrigerator for up to 1 week or stash them in the freezer.

NUTRITION FACTS	Amount Per Serving	%Daily Value*
	Total Fat 8g	Total Carbohydrate 8g
Serving Size 1 bar	Saturated Fat 7g	Dietary Fiber 5g
Servings Per Recipe 10	Trans Fat 0g	Sugars 2g
Calories 170	Cholesterol 0mg	Protein 14g
Calories from Fat 70	Sodium 85mg	
*Percent Daily Value are based on a 2,000 calorie diet.	Vitamin A 0% Vitamin C 0% Calcium 6%	Iron 10%

SUNFLOWER SEED PROTEIN BARS

MAKES 10 PROTEIN BARS

128g (½ cup) **Toasted Sunflower Seed Butter**

1 cup + 2 tablespoons **Unsweetened Vanilla Almond Milk**

1 teaspoon **Vanilla Crème-Flavored Liquid Stevia Extract**

168g (1¼ cups, lightly packed) **Vanilla Brown Rice Protein Powder**

80g (⅔ cup) **Oat Flour**

¼ teaspoon **Salt**

1 tablespoon **Hulled Sunflower Seeds**

1. Line an 8x8" brownie pan with parchment paper. Set aside.

2. In an electric stand mixer bowl fitted with a beater attachment, add all of the ingredients. Mix on low speed until everything is fully incorporated.

3. Scrape down the sides of the bowl. Mix on medium speed for one last mix. Mixture should be thick and fudgy, like cookie dough.

4. Scoop the mixture into the brownie pan and flatten it out. Tightly cover the pan with plastic wrap and refrigerate overnight.

5. Lift the mixture out of the pan. Slice into 10 bars. Individually wrap the protein bars in plastic sandwich baggies. Store in the refrigerator for up to 1 week or stash them in the freezer.

NUTRITION FACTS

Serving Size 1 bar
Servings Per Recipe 10
Calories 190
 Calories from Fat 80

*Percent Daily Value are based on a 2,000 calorie diet.

Amount Per Serving		%Daily Value*
Total Fat 9g	Total Carbohydrate 11g	
Saturated Fat 1g	Dietary Fiber 3g	
Trans Fat 0g	Sugars 1g	
Cholesterol 0mg	Protein 16g	
Sodium 130mg		
Vitamin A 0% Vitamin C 0% Calcium 10%		Iron 15%

PUMPKIN SEED PROTEIN BARS

MAKES 10 PROTEIN BARS

128g (½ cup) **Toasted Pumpkin Seed Butter**

1 cup + 2 tablespoons **Unsweetened Vanilla Almond Milk**

1 teaspoon **Vanilla Crème-Flavored Liquid Stevia Extract**

168g (1¼ cups, lightly packed) **Vanilla Brown Rice Protein Powder**

80g (⅔ cup) **Oat Flour**

⅛ teaspoon **Salt**

2 tablespoons **Toasted Pumpkin Seeds,**

1. Line an 8x8" brownie pan with parchment paper. Set aside.

2. In an electric stand mixer bowl fitted with a beater attachment, add all of the ingredients. Mix on low speed until everything is fully incorporated.

3. Scrape down the sides of the bowl. Mix on medium speed for one last mix. Mixture should be thick and fudgy, like cookie dough.

4. Scoop the mixture into the brownie pan and flatten it out. Tightly cover the pan with plastic wrap and refrigerate overnight

5. Lift the mixture out of the pan. Slice into 10 bars. Individually wrap the protein bars in plastic sandwich baggies. Store in the refrigerator for up to 1 week or stash them in the freezer.

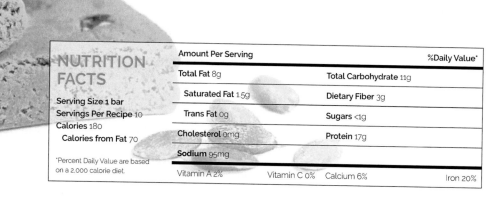

NUTRITION FACTS	Amount Per Serving		%Daily Value*
Serving Size 1 bar	Total Fat 8g	Total Carbohydrate 11g	
Servings Per Recipe 10	Saturated Fat 1.5g	Dietary Fiber 3g	
Calories 180	Trans Fat 0g	Sugars <1g	
Calories from Fat 70	Cholesterol 0mg	Protein 17g	
*Percent Daily Value are based on a 2,000 calorie diet.	Sodium 95mg		
	Vitamin A 2%	Vitamin C 0% Calcium 6%	Iron 20%

PROTEIN POWDER-FREE PROTEIN BARS

MAKES 12 PROTEIN BARS

15oz can **Garbanzo Beans (Chickpeas),** **unseasoned**

245g (1 cup) **Unsweetened Applesauce**

210g (1½ cups) **Raisins**

128g (½ cup) **Natural Peanut Butter**

1 tablespoon **Pure Vanilla Extract**

200g (1¾ cups) **Quick-Cooking Oats**

56g (½ cup) **Ground Flaxseed Meal**

2 teaspoons **Ground Cinnamon**

¼ teaspoon **Salt**

1. Line a 9x9" brownie pan with parchment paper. Set aside.

2. Drain the can of garbanzo beans and pour the beans into a sieve. Rinse well and drain off excess water (should yield 1½ cups).

3. In a food processor, add all of the ingredients. Blend until everything is fully incorporated.

4. Scrape down the sides of the food processor. Blend again to make sure the mixture is even (you don't wanna chomp down on a whole chickpea!). Let the dough sit for 15 minutes to thicken. If it seems too sticky or wet, mix in more oats or flaxseed meal (chia seeds can work too!).

5. Scoop the mixture into the brownie pan and flatten it out. Tightly cover the pan with plastic wrap and refrigerate overnight.

6. Lift the mixture out of the pan. Slice into 12 bars. Individually wrap the protein bars in plastic sandwich baggies. Store in the refrigerator for up to 1 week or stash them in the freezer.

NUTRITION FACTS	Amount Per Serving		%Daily Value*
	Total Fat 9g	Total Carbohydrate 34g	
	Saturated Fat 1g	Dietary Fiber 6g	
Serving Size 1 bar	Trans Fat 0g	Sugars 15g	
Servings Per Recipe 12			
Calories 240	Cholesterol 0mg	Protein 8g	
Calories from Fat 80			
	Sodium 55mg		
*Percent Daily Value are based on a 2,000 calorie diet.	Vitamin A 0% Vitamin C 4%	Calcium 4%	Iron 10%

MORE FLAVOR IDEAS

Follow the **Sunflower Seed Protein Bar** recipe and...

BRAZIL NUT BUTTER PROTEIN BARS
... swap the Sunflower Seed Butter with Brazil Nut Butter!

CASHEW BUTTER PROTEIN BARS
... swap the Sunflower Seed Butter with Cashew Butter!

PECAN BUTTER PROTEIN BARS
... swap the Sunflower Seed Butter with Pecan Butter! Feel free to add some spices (like cinnamon and nutmeg) and replace 2 tablespoons of almond milk with pure maple syrup.

PISTACHIO BUTTER PROTEIN BARS
... swap the Sunflower Seed Butter with Pistachio Butter!

MACADAMIA NUT BUTTER PROTEIN BARS
... swap the Sunflower Seed Butter with Macadamia Butter!

WALNUT BUTTER PROTEIN BARS
... swap the Sunflower Seed Butter with Walnut Butter! Feel free to add some spices (like cinnamon and nutmeg) and replace 2 tablespoons of almond milk with pure maple syrup.

HEMP SEED BUTTER PROTEIN BARS
... swap the Sunflower Seed Butter with Hemp Seed Butter!

TAHINI (SESAME SEED BUTTER) PROTEIN BARS
... swap the Sunflower Seed Butter with Tahini!

FRUITY FLAVORS

RASPBERRY ALMOND 15

ORANGE CRANBERRY 18

CHOCOLATE-COVERED
STRAWBERRY 19

CARAMEL APPLE 21

CHERRY PIE 24

BANANA BREAD 25

BLUEBERRY MUFFIN 28

RASPBERRY ALMOND PROTEIN BARS

MAKES 10 PROTEIN BARS

85g (⅓ cup) **Roasted Almond Butter**

1 cup **Unsweetened Vanilla Almond Milk**

2 tablespoons **Beet Juice, from a can of sliced beets**

¾ teaspoon **Vanilla Crème-Flavored Liquid Stevia Extract**

¾ teaspoon **Raspberry Flavor**

¾ teaspoon **Almond Extract**

135g (1 cup, lightly packed) **Vanilla Brown Rice Protein Powder**

120g (1 cup) **Oat Flour**

⅛ teaspoon **Salt**

½ cup **Freeze-Dried Raspberries, ground into a powder** (measure after grinding)

1. Line an 8x8" brownie pan with parchment paper. Set aside.

2. In an electric stand mixer bowl fitted with a beater attachment, add all of the ingredients. Mix on low speed until everything is fully incorporated. Feel free to sift the raspberry powder through a fine mesh sieve if you want to avoid the seeds.

3. Scrape down the sides of the bowl. Mix on medium speed for one last mix. Mixture should be thick and fudgy, like cookie dough.

4. Scoop the mixture into the brownie pan and flatten it out. Tightly cover the pan with plastic wrap and refrigerate overnight.

5. Lift the mixture out of the pan. Slice into 10 bars. Individually wrap the protein bars in plastic sandwich baggies. Store in the refrigerator for up to 1 week or stash them in the freezer.

NUTRITION FACTS	Amount Per Serving	%Daily Value*
	Total Fat 5.5g	Total Carbohydrate 15g
Serving Size 1 bar	Saturated Fat 0.5g	Dietary Fiber 4g
Servings Per Recipe 10	Trans Fat 0g	Sugars 2g
Calories 170	Cholesterol 0mg	Protein 13.5g
Calories from Fat 50	Sodium 80mg	
*Percent Daily Value are based on a 2,000 calorie diet.	Vitamin A 0% Vitamin C 10% Calcium 10%	Iron 15%

ORANGE CRANBERRY PROTEIN BARS

MAKES 10 PROTEIN BARS

85g (⅓ cup) **Roasted Almond Butter**

1 cup + 2 tablespoons **Unsweetened Vanilla Almond Milk**

1 tablespoon **Orange Zest**

1½ teaspoons **Vanilla Crème-Flavored Liquid Stevia Extract**

168g (1¼ cups, lightly packed) **Vanilla Brown Rice Protein Powder**

90g (¾ cup) **Oat Flour**

26g (¼ cup) **Quinoa Flakes**

⅛ teaspoon **Salt**

⅔ cup **Dried Cranberries, chopped**

1. Line an 8x8" brownie pan with parchment paper. Set aside.

2. In an electric stand mixer bowl fitted with a beater attachment, add all of the ingredients. Mix on low speed until everything is fully incorporated.

3. Scrape down the sides of the bowl. Mix on medium speed for one last mix. Mixture should be thick and fudgy, like cookie dough.

4. Scoop the mixture into the brownie pan and flatten it out. Tightly cover the pan with plastic wrap and refrigerate overnight.

5. Lift the mixture out of the pan. Slice into 10 bars. Individually wrap the protein bars in plastic sandwich baggies. Store in the refrigerator for up to 1 week or stash them in the freezer.

NOTES: 1) You may substitute the quinoa flakes for quick-cooking oats. 2) I use dried cranberries that are sweetened with apple juice, not sugar. Any kind of dried cranberries will work, though!

NUTRITION FACTS	Amount Per Serving		%Daily Value*
	Total Fat 5.5g	Total Carbohydrate 17g	
Serving Size 1 bar	Saturated Fat 0g	Dietary Fiber 4g	
Servings Per Recipe 10	Trans Fat 0g	Sugars 5g	
Calories 180	Cholesterol 0mg	Protein 16g	
Calories from Fat 50	Sodium 95mg		
*Percent Daily Value are based on a 2,000 calorie diet.	Vitamin A 0%	Vitamin C 0% Calcium 8%	Iron 15%

CHOCOLATE-COVERED STRAWBERRY PROTEIN BARS

MAKES 12 PROTEIN BARS

PROTEIN BARS

85g (⅓ cup) **Roasted Almond Butter**

¾ cup **Unsweetened Vanilla Almond Milk**

2 tablespoons **Beet Juice, from a can of beets**

1 teaspoon **Strawberry Flavor**

¾ teaspoon **Vanilla Crème-Flavored Liquid Stevia Extract**

168g (1¼ cups, lightly packed) **Vanilla Brown Rice Protein Powder**

¾ cup **Freeze-Dried Strawberries, ground into a powder** (measure after grinding)

27g (3 tablespoons) **Coconut Flour**

⅛ teaspoon **Salt**

CHOCOLATE COATING

6oz **Bittersweet Chocolate (70% cacao), melted**

NUTRITION FACTS	Amount Per Serving		%Daily Value*
	Total Fat 10g	**Total Carbohydrate** 17g	
Serving Size 1 bar	Saturated Fat 4g	Dietary Fiber 5g	
Servings Per Recipe 12			
Calories 210	**Trans Fat** 0g	Sugars 9g	
Calories from Fat 90	**Cholesterol** 0mg	**Protein** 14g	
*Percent Daily Value are based on a 2,000 calorie diet.	**Sodium** 75mg		
	Vitamin A 0%	Vitamin C 0% Calcium 6%	Iron 15%

FOR THE PROTEIN BARS

1. Line an 8x8" brownie pan with parchment paper. Set aside.

2. In an electric stand mixer bowl fitted with a beater attachment, add all of the ingredients. Mix on low speed until everything is fully incorporated.

3. Scrape down the sides of the bowl. Mix on medium speed for one last mix. Mixture should be thick and fudgy, like cookie dough.

4. Scoop the mixture into the brownie pan and flatten it out. Tightly cover the pan with plastic wrap and refrigerate overnight.

5. Lift the mixture out of the pan. Slice into 12 bars.

FOR THE CHOCOLATE COATING

6. Place a silicone baking mat on top of a jelly roll pan and line the protein bars on top. With a large spoon, ladle the melted chocolate over the protein bars. Try to encase the entire protein bar with chocolate, but it doesn't have to be perfect.

7. Refrigerate until firm (~1 hour). Individually wrap the protein bars in plastic sandwich baggies. Store in the refrigerator for up to 1 week or stash them in the freezer.

CARAMEL APPLE PROTEIN BARS

MAKES 10 PROTEIN BARS

PROTEIN BARS

262g (1 cup + 1 tablespoon) **Unsweetened Applesauce**

85g (⅓ cup) **Roasted Cashew Butter**

1 teaspoon **Vanilla Crème-Flavored Liquid Stevia Extract**

1 teaspoon **Natural Butter Flavor**

168g (1¼ cups, lightly packed) **Vanilla Brown Rice Protein Powder**

40g (⅓ cup) **Oat Flour**

34g (⅓ cup) **Quinoa Flakes**

1 tablespoon **Ground Cinnamon**

¼ teaspoon **Salt**

CARAMEL LAYER

⅓ cup **Organic Caramel Sauce** (see Pantry Staples on pg. ix)

75g (½ cup, packed) **Vanilla Brown Rice Protein Powder**

FOR THE PROTEIN BARS

1. Line an 8x8" brownie pan with parchment paper. Set aside.

2. In an electric stand mixer bowl fitted with a beater attachment, add all of the ingredients. Mix on low speed until everything is fully incorporated.

3. Scrape down the sides of the bowl. Mix on medium speed for one last mix. Mixture should be thick and fudgy, like cookie dough.

4. Scoop the mixture into the brownie pan and flatten it out.

FOR THE CARAMEL LAYER

5. In a small bowl, stir together the caramel sauce and protein powder. Mixture should be like a thick, slightly sticky frosting. Spoon the mixture over the protein bar base and spread to the edges of the pan (I used an offset spatula). Place in the freezer uncovered for 1 hour.

6. Lift the mixture out of the pan. Slice into 10 bars. To store, simply place a sheet of parchment paper on top of a cake pedestal, arrange the protein bars on top, and cover with a cake dome (keeps for ~1 week).

NUTRITION FACTS	Amount Per Serving		%Daily Value*
	Total Fat 5g	**Total Carbohydrate** 21g	
Serving Size 1 bar	**Saturated Fat** 1.5g	**Dietary Fiber** 4g	
Servings Per Recipe 10	**Trans Fat** 0g	**Sugars** 10g	
Calories 210	**Cholesterol** 0mg	**Protein** 20g	
Calories from Fat 45	**Sodium** 130mg		
*Percent Daily Value are based on a 2,000 calorie diet.	Vitamin A 0% Vitamin C 6%	Calcium 4%	Iron 15%

CHERRY PIE PROTEIN BARS

MAKES 10 PROTEIN BARS

85g (⅓ cup) **Raw Almond Butter**

1 cup **Unsweetened Vanilla Almond Milk**

1 teaspoon **Cherry Flavor**

¾ teaspoon **Vanilla Crème-Flavored Liquid Stevia Extract**

1⅓ cups **Freeze-Dried Cherries, ground into a powder** (measure after grinding)

168g (1¼ cups, lightly packed) **Vanilla Brown Rice Protein Powder**

30g (¼ cup) **Oat Flour**

¼ teaspoon **Salt**

1. Line an 8x8" brownie pan with parchment paper. Set aside.

2. In an electric stand mixer bowl fitted with a beater attachment, add all of the ingredients. Mix on low speed until everything is fully incorporated.

3. Scrape down the sides of the bowl. Mix on medium speed for one last mix. Mixture should be thick and fudgy, like cookie dough.

4. Scoop the mixture into the brownie pan and flatten it out. Tightly cover the pan with plastic wrap and refrigerate overnight.

5. Lift the mixture out of the pan. Slice into 10 bars. Individually wrap the protein bars in plastic sandwich baggies. Store in the refrigerator for up to 1 week or stash them in the freezer.

NUTRITION FACTS	Amount Per Serving		%Daily Value*
	Total Fat 4.5g	Total Carbohydrate 20g	
Serving Size 1 bar	Saturated Fat 0g	Dietary Fiber 4g	
Servings Per Recipe 10	Trans Fat 0g	Sugars 12g	
Calories 190	Cholesterol 0mg	Protein 16g	
Calories from Fat 45	Sodium 140mg		
*Percent Daily Value are based on a 2,000 calorie diet.	Vitamin A 15%	Vitamin C 4%	Calcium 10%	Iron 15%

BANANA BREAD PROTEIN BARS

MAKES 10 PROTEIN BARS

85g (⅓ cup) **Roasted Walnut Butter (Roasted Almond Butter works great too!**

1 cup **Unsweetened Vanilla Almond Milk**

1 teaspoon **Vanilla Crème-Flavored Liquid Stevia Extract**

1 teaspoon **Banana Flavor**

1 teaspoon **Natural Butter Flavor**

168g (1¼ cups, lightly packed) **Vanilla Brown Rice Protein Powder**

3.5oz (1½ cups) **Freeze-Dried Bananas**

40g (⅓ cup) **Oat Flour**

1 tablespoon **Ground Cinnamon**

¼ teaspoon **Salt**

1. Line an 8x8" brownie pan with parchment paper. Set aside.

2. In an electric stand mixer bowl fitted with a beater attachment, add all of the ingredients. Mix on low speed until everything is fully incorporated. Feel free to add ¼ cup of chopped walnuts!

3. Scrape down the sides of the bowl. Mix on medium speed for one last mix. Mixture should be thick and fudgy, like cookie dough, but with small chunks of banana throughout.

4. Scoop the mixture into the brownie pan and flatten it out. Tightly cover the pan with plastic wrap and refrigerate overnight.

5. Lift the mixture out of the pan. Slice into 10 bars. Individually wrap the protein bars in plastic sandwich baggies. Store in the refrigerator for up to 1 week or stash them in the freezer.

NUTRITION FACTS	Amount Per Serving	%Daily Value*
Serving Size **1 bar**	Total Fat 6g	Total Carbohydrate 17g
Servings Per Recipe 10	Saturated Fat 0.5g	Dietary Fiber 4g
Calories 180	Trans Fat 0g	Sugars 8g
Calories from Fat 50	Cholesterol 0mg	Protein 14g
	Sodium 120mg	
*Percent Daily Value are based on a 2,000 calorie diet.	Vitamin A 0% Vitamin C 0% Calcium 6%	Iron 10%

BLUEBERRY MUFFIN PROTEIN BARS

MAKES 10 PROTEIN BARS

85g (⅓ cup) **Roasted Walnut Butter**

1 cup + 2 tablespoons **Unsweetened Vanilla Almond Milk**

1 teaspoon **Lemon Zest**

1 teaspoon **Natural Butter Flavor**

1 teaspoon **Vanilla Crème-Flavored Liquid Stevia Extract**

¾ teaspoon **Blueberry Flavor**

168g (1¼ cups, lightly packed) **Vanilla Brown Rice Protein Powder**

80g (⅔ cup) **Oat Flour**

¼ cup **Quick-Cooking Oats**

¼ teaspoon **Salt**

¾ cup **Dried Blueberries**

1. Line an 8x8" brownie pan with parchment paper. Set aside.

2. In an electric stand mixer bowl fitted with a beater attachment, add all of the ingredients. Mix on low speed until everything is fully incorporated. Feel free to add ¼ cup of chopped walnuts!

3. Scrape down the sides of the bowl. Mix on medium speed for one last mix. Mixture should be thick and fudgy, like cookie dough.

4. Scoop the mixture into the brownie pan and flatten it out. Tightly cover the pan with plastic wrap and refrigerate overnight.

5. Lift the mixture out of the pan. Slice into 10 bars. Individually wrap the protein bars in plastic sandwich baggies. Store in the refrigerator for up to 1 week or stash them in the freezer.

NOTE: I use dried blueberries with no sugar added. Any kind of dried blueberries will work, though!

NUTRITION FACTS	Amount Per Serving		%Daily Value*
	Total Fat 7g	Total Carbohydrate 20g	
Serving Size 1 bar	Saturated Fat 0.5g	Dietary Fiber 4g	
Servings Per Recipe 10	Trans Fat 0g	Sugars 5g	
Calories 200	Cholesterol 0mg	Protein 16g	
Calories from Fat 60	Sodium 110mg		
*Percent Daily Value are based on a 2,000 calorie diet.	Vitamin A 0%	Vitamin C 0% Calcium 10%	Iron 15%

BAKED FLAVORS

COOKIE DOUGH 31

OATMEAL RAISIN COOKIE · 34

WHITE CHOCOLATE
MACADAMIA COOKIE 37

RED VELVET CAKE 40

UNBAKED CINNAMON
ROLL 41

GERMAN CHOCOLATE 43
CAKE

BAKED FLAVORS

BIRTHDAY CAKE 46

CARROT CAKE 47

SEVEN SINS 50

PUMPKIN PIE 51

PECAN PIE 54

TIRAMISÙ 55

COOKIE DOUGH PROTEIN BARS

MAKES 10 PROTEIN BARS

128g (½ cup) **Roasted Almond Butter**

¾ cup + 3 tablespoons **Unsweetened Vanilla Almond Milk**

1¼ teaspoons **Vanilla Crème-Flavored Liquid Stevia Extract**

1 teaspoon **Natural Butter Flavor**

168g (1¼ cups, lightly packed) **Vanilla Brown Rice Protein Powder**

90g (¾ cup) **Oat Flour**

¼ teaspoon **Salt**

¼ cup **No-Sugar-Added Chocolate Chips (or Mini Semi-Sweet Chocolate Chips)**

1. Line an 8x8" brownie pan with parchment paper. Set aside.

2. In an electric stand mixer bowl fitted with a beater attachment, add all of the ingredients. Mix on low speed until everything is fully incorporated.

3. Scrape down the sides of the bowl. Mix on medium speed for one last mix. Mixture should be thick and fudgy, like cookie dough.

4. Scoop the mixture into the brownie pan and flatten it out. Tightly cover the pan with plastic wrap and refrigerate overnight.

5. Lift the mixture out of the pan. Slice into 10 bars. Individually wrap the protein bars in plastic sandwich baggies. Store in the refrigerator for up to 1 week or stash them in the freezer.

NUTRITION FACTS	Amount Per Serving	%Daily Value*
	Total Fat 8g	Total Carbohydrate 13g
	Saturated Fat 1.5g	Dietary Fiber 4g
Serving Size 1 bar	Trans Fat 0g	Sugars <1g
Servings Per Recipe 10	Cholesterol 0mg	Protein 17g
Calories 190	Sodium 115mg	
Calories from Fat 80		
*Percent Daily Value are based on a 2,000 calorie diet.	Vitamin A 0% Vitamin C 0% Calcium 8%	Iron 15%

OATMEAL RAISIN PROTEIN COOKIES & BALLS

MAKES 9 PROTEIN COOKIES + 6 PROTEIN BALLS

128g (½ cup) **Roasted Walnut Butter (Roasted Almond Butter works great too!)**

1 cup **Unsweetened Vanilla Almond Milk**

1 teaspoon **Vanilla Crème-Flavored Liquid Stevia Extract**

1 teaspoon **Natural Butter Flavor**

168g (1¼ cups, lightly packed) **Vanilla Brown Rice Protein Powder**

60g (½ cup) **Oat Flour**

⅓ cup **Quick-Cooking Oats**

⅓ cup **Raisins, chopped**

1½ teaspoons **Ground Cinnamon**

¼ teaspoon **Salt**

1. Line an 8x8" brownie pan with parchment paper. Set aside.

2. In an electric stand mixer bowl fitted with a beater attachment, add all of the ingredients. Mix on low speed until everything is fully incorporated.

3. Scrape down the sides of the bowl. Mix on medium speed for one last mix. Mixture should be thick and fudgy, like cookie dough.

4. Scoop the mixture into the brownie pan and flatten it out. Tightly cover the pan with plastic wrap and refrigerate overnight.

5. Lift the mixture out of the pan. Use a circle cookie cutter to punch out 9 cookies (use a 2½" cutter with an 8" pan, or 2¾" cutter with a 9" pan). Use the remaining dough leftover after punching out the cookies to roll into protein balls (or you can snack on it straight!). Individually wrap the protein cookies in plastic sandwich baggies. Store in the refrigerator for up to 1 week or stash them in the freezer.

PROTEIN COOKIES

NUTRITION FACTS

Serving Size 1 cookie
Servings Per Recipe 9
Calories 170
  Calories from Fat 70

*Percent Daily Value are based on a 2,000 calorie diet.

Amount Per Serving	%Daily Value*
Total Fat 8g	Total Carbohydrate 13g
Saturated Fat 0.5g	Dietary Fiber 3g
Trans Fat 0g	Sugars 3g
Cholesterol 0mg	Protein 13g
Sodium 100mg	
Vitamin A 0% — Vitamin C 0% — Calcium 6%	Iron 10%

PROTEIN BALLS

NUTRITION FACTS

Serving Size 1 ball
Servings Per Recipe 6
Calories 90
  Calories from Fat 35

*Percent Daily Value are based on a 2,000 calorie diet.

Amount Per Serving	%Daily Value*
Total Fat 4g	Total Carbohydrate 6g
Saturated Fat 0g	Dietary Fiber 2g
Trans Fat 0g	Sugars 2g
Cholesterol 0mg	Protein 7g
Sodium 50mg	
Vitamin A 0% — Vitamin C 0% — Calcium 2%	Iron 6%

WHITE CHOCOLATE MACADAMIA PROTEIN COOKIES & BALLS

MAKES 9 PROTEIN COOKIES + 6 PROTEIN BALLS

PROTEIN COOKIES

128g (½ cup) **Roasted Macadamia Butter**

1 cup **Unsweetened Vanilla Almond Milk**

1 teaspoon **Vanilla Crème-Flavored Liquid Stevia Extract**

1 teaspoon **Natural Butter Flavor**

168g (1¼ cups, lightly packed) **Vanilla Brown Rice Protein Powder**

90g (¾ cup) **Oat Flour**

¼ teaspoon **Salt**

WHITE CHOCOLATE COATING

6oz **White Chocolate, melted**

1 tablespoon **Coconut Oil, melted**

PROTEIN COOKIES

NUTRITION FACTS	Amount Per Serving		%Daily Value*
	Total Fat 15g	**Total Carbohydrate** 17g	
Serving Size 1 cookie	Saturated Fat 5g	Dietary Fiber 3g	
Servings Per Recipe 9	Trans Fat 0g	Sugars 8g	
Calories 250	Cholesterol <5mg	**Protein** 13g	
Calories from Fat 140	**Sodium** 110mg		
*Percent Daily Value are based on a 2,000 calorie diet.	Vitamin A 0% Vitamin C 0% Calcium 10%		Iron 10%

PROTEIN BALLS

NUTRITION FACTS	Amount Per Serving		%Daily Value*
	Total Fat 7g	**Total Carbohydrate** 9g	
Serving Size 1 ball	Saturated Fat 2.5g	Dietary Fiber 2g	
Servings Per Recipe 6	Trans Fat 0g	Sugars 4g	
Calories 130	Cholesterol 0mg	**Protein** 7g	
Calories from Fat 70	**Sodium** 55mg		
*Percent Daily Value are based on a 2,000 calorie diet.	Vitamin A 0% Vitamin C 0% Calcium 6%		Iron 6%

FOR THE PROTEIN COOKIES

1. Line an 8x8" brownie pan (or 9x9" for thinner cookies) with parchment paper. Set aside.

2. In an electric stand mixer bowl fitted with a beater attachment, add all of the ingredients. Mix on low speed until everything is fully incorporated. Feel free to add a handful of chopped macadamia nuts!

3. Scrape down the sides of the bowl. Mix on medium speed for one last mix. Mixture should be thick and fudgy, like cookie dough.

4. Scoop the mixture into the brownie pan and flatten it out. Tightly cover the pan with plastic wrap and refrigerate overnight.

5. Lift the mixture out of the pan. Use a circle cookie cutter to punch out 9 cookies (use a 2½" cutter with an 8" pan, or 2¾" cutter with a 9" pan). Use the remaining dough leftover after punching out the cookies to roll into protein balls (or you can snack on it straight!).

FOR THE WHITE CHOCOLATE COATING

6. Stir the coconut oil into the melted white chocolate.

7. Place a silicone baking mat on top of a jelly roll pan and line the protein cookies on top. Place a protein cookie on the prongs of a large fork and dunk into the melted white chocolate. With a large spoon, ladle the chocolate over the cookie. Gently slide the cookie onto the silicone baking mat. Repeat this process with the rest of the protein cookies.

8. Refrigerate until firm (~2 hours). Individually wrap the protein cookies in plastic sandwich baggies. Store in the refrigerator for up to 1 week or stash them in the freezer.

NUTRITION FACTS

Serving Size 1 bar
Servings Per Recipe 12
Calories 250
  Calories from Fat 110

*Percent Daily Value are based on a 2,000 calorie diet.

Amount Per Serving		%Daily Value*
Total Fat 12g	**Total Carbohydrate** 16g	
Saturated Fat 4g	Dietary Fiber 5g	
Trans Fat 0g	Sugars 5g	
Cholesterol 0mg	**Protein** 19g	
Sodium 95mg		

Vitamin A 0%	Vitamin C 0%	Calcium 8%	Iron 25%

RED VELVET CAKE PROTEIN BARS

MAKES 12 PROTEIN BARS

PROTEIN BARS

165g (⅔ cup) **Roasted Beet Puree** (see Instructions)

128g (½ cup) **Raw Almond Butter** (Roasted Almond Butter works great too!)

½ cup **Unsweetened Vanilla Almond Milk**

1 tablespoon **Natural Butter Flavor**

1½ teaspoons **Vanilla Crème-Flavored Liquid Stevia Extract**

210g (1⅔ cups, lightly packed) **Chocolate Brown Rice Protein Powder**

80g (⅔ cup) **Oat Flour**

¼ teaspoon **Salt**

CHOCOLATE COATING

6oz **Bittersweet Chocolate (70% cacao), melted**

> NOTE: Using canned or prepackaged cooked beets will not provide the same vibrant red color as using freshly roasted beets… the bars will turn out brown (yes, I tried it). For best results, use freshly roasted beet puree!

FOR THE ROASTED BEET PUREE

1. Preheat your oven to 350 degrees Fahrenheit. Rinse and gently scrub two fist-sized beets. Wrap them completely in foil, place on a baking sheet, and bake for ~1½ hours, or until a fork pierces through with ease.

2. Let sit until it's cool enough to handle, then carefully unwrap the foil. Use a butter knife to scrape off the beet skins (they will fall off easily).

3. Chop the beets into chunks and place in a food processor. Puree until completely smooth.

FOR THE PROTEIN BARS

4. Line an 8x8" brownie pan with parchment paper. Set aside.

5. In an electric stand mixer bowl fitted with a beater attachment, add all of the ingredients. Mix on low speed until everything is fully incorporated.

6. Scrape down the sides of the bowl. Mix on medium speed for one last mix. Mixture should be thick and fudgy, like cookie dough.

7. Scoop the mixture into the brownie pan and flatten it out. Tightly cover the pan with plastic wrap and refrigerate overnight.

8. Lift the mixture out of the pan. Slice into 12 bars.

FOR THE CHOCOLATE COATING

9. Place a silicone baking mat on top of a jelly roll pan and line the protein bars on top. With a large spoon, ladle the melted chocolate over the protein bars. Try to encase the entire protein bar with chocolate, but it doesn't have to be perfect.

10. Refrigerate until firm (~1 hour). Individually wrap the protein bars in plastic sandwich baggies. Store in the refrigerator for up to 1 week or stash them in the freezer.

UNBAKED CINNAMON ROLL PROTEIN SQUARES

MAKES 9 PROTEIN SQUARES

PROTEIN SQUARES

128g (½ cup) **Roasted Almond Butter**

¾ cup + 3 tablespoons **Unsweetened Vanilla Almond Milk**

63g (3 tablespoons) **Pure Maple Syrup**

1 teaspoon **Natural Butter Flavor**

¾ teaspoon **Vanilla Crème-Flavored Liquid Stevia Extract**

168g (1¼ cups, lightly packed) **Vanilla Brown Rice Protein Powder**

90g (¾ cup) **Oat Flour**

2 teaspoons **Ground Cinnamon**

¼ teaspoon **Salt**

CREAM CHEESE FROSTING

4oz **Neufchâtel Cream Cheese, room temperature (or ⅓ Less Fat Cream Cheese)**

1-2 tablespoons **Unsweetened Vanilla Almond Milk**

¼ teaspoon **Vanilla Crème-Flavored Liquid Stevia Extract**

¼ teaspoon **Natural Butter Flavor**

⅛ teaspoon **Vanilla Bean Paste**

FOR THE PROTEIN SQUARES

1. Line an 8x8" brownie pan with parchment paper. Set aside.

2. In an electric stand mixer bowl fitted with a beater attachment, add all of the ingredients. Mix on low speed until everything is fully incorporated.

3. Scrape down the sides of the bowl. Mix on medium speed for one last mix. Mixture should be thick and fudgy, like cookie dough.

4. Scoop the mixture into the brownie pan and flatten it out. Tightly cover the pan with plastic wrap and refrigerate overnight.

5. Lift the mixture out of the pan. Slice into 9 squares.

FOR THE CREAM CHEESE FROSTING

6. In a medium-sized mixing bowl, whisk together the cream cheese, almond milk, stevia extract, butter flavor and vanilla paste. Spread the frosting over the squares. To store, simply place a sheet of parchment paper on top of a cake pedestal, arrange the protein squares on top, and cover with a cake dome (keeps for ~1 week).

NUTRITION FACTS

Serving Size 1 square
Servings Per Recipe 9
Calories 240
   Calories from Fat 100

*Percent Daily Value are based on a 2,000 calorie diet.

Amount Per Serving		%Daily Value*
Total Fat 11g	**Total Carbohydrate** 18g	
Saturated Fat 2.5g	Dietary Fiber 4g	
Trans Fat 0g	Sugars 6g	
Cholesterol 10mg	Protein 19g	
Sodium 180mg		
Vitamin A 2%	Vitamin C 0%	Calcium 10%	Iron 15%

GERMAN CHOCOLATE CAKE PROTEIN BARS

MAKES 12 PROTEIN BARS

PROTEIN BARS

128g (½ cup) **Roasted Pecan Butter**
(Roasted Almond Butter works great too!)

1 cup + 2 tablespoons **Unsweetened Vanilla Almond Milk**

1 teaspoon **Vanilla Crème-Flavored Liquid Stevia Extract**

168g (1¼ cups, lightly packed) **Chocolate Brown Rice Protein Powder**

80g (⅔ cup) **Oat Flour**

2 tablespoons **Unsweetened Natural Cocoa Powder**

½ teaspoon **Espresso Powder**

¼ teaspoon **Salt**

TOPPINGS

2oz **Bittersweet Chocolate (70% cacao), melted**

2 tablespoons **Reduced Fat Unsweetened Shredded Coconut**

2 tablespoons **Roasted Pecans, chopped**

FOR THE PROTEIN BARS

1. Line an 8x8" brownie pan with parchment paper. Set aside.

2. In an electric stand mixer bowl fitted with a beater attachment, add all of the ingredients. Mix on low speed until everything is fully incorporated.

3. Scrape down the sides of the bowl. Mix on medium speed for one last mix. Mixture should be thick and fudgy, like cookie dough.

4. Scoop the mixture into the brownie pan and flatten it out. Tightly cover the pan with plastic wrap and refrigerate overnight.

5. Lift the mixture out of the pan. Slice into 12 bars.

FOR THE TOPPINGS

6. Place a silicone baking mat on top of a jelly roll pan and line the protein bars on top. Spread the melted chocolate over the protein bars, sprinkle with the shredded coconut, and press the chopped pecans on top.

7. Refrigerate until firm (~1 hour). Individually wrap the protein bars in plastic sandwich baggies. Store in the refrigerator for up to 1 week or stash them in the freezer.

NUTRITION FACTS	Amount Per Serving	%Daily Value*
	Total Fat 11g	**Total Carbohydrate** 10g
Serving Size 1 bar	Saturated Fat 2g	Dietary Fiber 4g
Servings Per Recipe 12	Trans Fat 0g	Sugars 2g
Calories 190	**Cholesterol** 0mg	**Protein** 14g
Calories from Fat 100	**Sodium** 95mg	
*Percent Daily Value are based on a 2,000 calorie diet.	Vitamin A 0% Vitamin C 0% Calcium 10%	Iron 15%

NUTRITION FACTS

Serving Size 1 bar
Servings Per Recipe 12
Calories 200
  Calories from Fat 80

*Percent Daily Value are based on a 2,000 calorie diet.

Amount Per Serving			%Daily Value*
Total Fat 8g		Total Carbohydrate 16g	
Saturated Fat 2g		Dietary Fiber 3g	
Trans Fat 0g		Sugars 4g	
Cholesterol 5mg		Protein 15g	
Sodium 140mg			
Vitamin A 0%	Vitamin C 0%	Calcium 8%	Iron 10%

BIRTHDAY CAKE PROTEIN BARS

MAKES 12 PROTEIN BARS

PROTEIN BARS

128g (½ cup) **Raw Almond Butter**

1 cup + 2 tablespoons **Unsweetened Vanilla Almond Milk**

2 teaspoons **Natural Butter Flavor**

1 teaspoon **Vanilla Crème-Flavored Liquid Stevia Extract**

¾ teaspoon **Almond Extract**

168g (1¼ cups, lightly packed) **Vanilla Brown Rice Protein Powder**

120g (1 cup) **Oat Flour**

¼ teaspoon **Salt**

CREAM CHEESE FROSTING

4oz **Neufchâtel Cream Cheese, room temperature (or ⅓ Less Fat Cream Cheese)**

2 tablespoons **Unsweetened Vanilla Almond Milk**

½ teaspoon **Vanilla Crème-Flavored Liquid Stevia Extract**

¼ cup **Natural Rainbow Sprinkles**

FOR THE PROTEIN BARS

1. Line an 8x8" brownie pan with parchment paper. Set aside.

2. In an electric stand mixer bowl fitted with a beater attachment, add all of the ingredients. Mix on low speed until everything is fully incorporated.

3. Scrape down the sides of the bowl. Mix on medium speed for one last mix. Mixture should be thick and fudgy, like cookie dough.

4. Scoop the mixture into the brownie pan and flatten it out.

FOR THE CREAM CHEESE FROSTING

5. In a medium-sized mixing bowl, whisk together the cream cheese, almond milk and stevia extract. Scoop mixture over the protein bar base and spread to the edges of the pan (I used an offset spatula). Place in the freezer uncovered for 1 hour.

6. Lift the mixture out of the pan. Slice into 12 bars.

7. Scatter the sprinkles on top. To store, simply place a sheet of parchment paper on top of a cake pedestal, arrange the protein bars on top, and cover with a cake dome (keeps for ~1 week).

CARROT CAKE PROTEIN BARS

MAKES 12 PROTEIN BARS

128g (½ cup) **Roasted Walnut Butter (Roasted Almond Butter works great too!)**

¾ cup + 2 tablespoons **Unsweetened Vanilla Almond Milk**

¾ teaspoon **Vanilla Crème-Flavored Liquid Stevia Extract**

168g (1¼ cups, lightly packed) **Vanilla Brown Rice Protein Powder**

90g (¾ cup) **Oat Flour**

1¾ teaspoons **Ground Cinnamon**

¼ teaspoon **Ground Nutmeg**

¼ teaspoon **Salt**

1½ cups **Grated Carrots**

⅓ cup **Reduced Fat Unsweetened Shredded Coconut**

¼ cup **Raisins, chopped**

1. Line a 9x9" brownie pan with parchment paper. Set aside.

2. In an electric stand mixer bowl fitted with a beater attachment, add all of the ingredients. Mix on low speed until everything is fully incorporated.

3. Scrape down the sides of the bowl. Mix on medium speed for one last mix. Mixture should be thick and fudgy, like cookie dough.

4. Scoop the mixture into the brownie pan and flatten it out. Tightly cover the pan with plastic wrap and refrigerate overnight.

5. Lift the mixture out of the pan. Slice into 12 bars. Individually wrap the protein bars in plastic sandwich baggies. Store in the refrigerator for up to 1 week or stash them in the freezer. **If you're craving a little more decadence, consider topping these with Cream Cheese Frosting (pg. 41)!**

NUTRITION FACTS	Amount Per Serving	%Daily Value*
	Total Fat 8g	Total Carbohydrate 14g
Serving Size 1 bar	Saturated Fat 1g	Dietary Fiber 4g
Servings Per Recipe 12	Trans Fat 0g	Sugars 4g
Calories 180	Cholesterol 0mg	Protein 13g
Calories from Fat 70	Sodium 95mg	
*Percent Daily Value are based on a 2,000 calorie diet.	Vitamin A 60% Vitamin C 0% Calcium 6%	Iron 10%

SEVEN SINS PROTEIN BARS

Like a Seven Layer Bar transformed into a protein bar!

MAKES 12 PROTEIN BARS

128g (½ cup) **Roasted Pecan Butter**

1 cup **Unsweetened Vanilla Almond Milk**

1 teaspoon **Natural Butterscotch Flavor**

½ teaspoon **English Toffee-Flavored Liquid Stevia Extract**

168g (1¼ cups, lightly packed) **Vanilla Brown Rice Protein Powder**

80g (⅔ cup) **Oat Flour**

½ cup **Reduced Fat Unsweetened Shredded Coconut**

½ cup **Mini Semi-Sweet Chocolate Chips**

½ cup **Graham Cracker Crumbs**

¼ teaspoon **Salt**

1. Line an 8x8" brownie pan with parchment paper. Set aside.

2. In an electric stand mixer bowl fitted with a beater attachment, add all of the ingredients. Mix on low speed until everything is fully incorporated.

3. Scrape down the sides of the bowl. Mix on medium speed for one last mix. Mixture should be thick and fudgy, like cookie dough.

4. Scoop the mixture into the brownie pan and flatten it out. Tightly cover the pan with plastic wrap and refrigerate overnight.

5. Lift the mixture out of the pan. Slice into 12 bars. Individually wrap the protein bars in plastic sandwich baggies. Store in the refrigerator for up to 1 week or stash them in the freezer.

NUTRITION FACTS	Amount Per Serving	%Daily Value*
	Total Fat 12g	Total Carbohydrate 16g
Serving Size 1 bar	Saturated Fat 3g	Dietary Fiber 4g
Servings Per Recipe 12	Trans Fat 0g	Sugars 6g
Calories 220	Cholesterol 0mg	Protein 13g
Calories from Fat 110	Sodium 130mg	
*Percent Daily Value are based on a 2,000 calorie diet.	Vitamin A 0% Vitamin C 0% Calcium 6%	Iron 15%

PUMPKIN PIE PROTEIN BARS

MAKES 12 PROTEIN BARS

one 15oz can **100% Pure Pumpkin Puree**

128g (½ cup) **Roasted Almond Butter**

2 teaspoons **Pure Vanilla Extract**

¾ teaspoon **English Toffee-Flavored Liquid Stevia Extract**

1¾ cups **Graham Cracker Crumbs**

168g (1¼ cups, lightly packed) **Vanilla Brown Rice Protein Powder**

1 tablespoon **Ground Cinnamon (or a mix of Ground Cinnamon + Pumpkin Pie Spice)**

⅛ teaspoon **Salt**

1. Line a 9x9" brownie pan with parchment paper. Set aside.

2. In an electric stand mixer bowl fitted with a beater attachment, add all of the ingredients. Mix on low speed until everything is fully incorporated.

3. Scrape down the sides of the bowl. Mix on medium speed for one last mix. Mixture should be thick and fudgy, like cookie dough.

4. Scoop the mixture into the brownie pan and flatten it out. Tightly cover the pan with plastic wrap and refrigerate overnight.

5. Lift the mixture out of the pan. Slice into 12 bars. Individually wrap the protein bars in plastic sandwich baggies. Store in the refrigerator for up to 1 week or stash them in the freezer.

NUTRITION FACTS	Amount Per Serving		%Daily Value*
	Total Fat 7g	Total Carbohydrate 20g	
Serving Size 1 bar	Saturated Fat 0g	Dietary Fiber 5g	
Servings Per Recipe 12	Trans Fat 0g	Sugars 5g	
Calories 200	Cholesterol 0mg	Protein 14g	
Calories from Fat 60	Sodium 180mg		
*Percent Daily Value are based on a 2,000 calorie diet.	Vitamin A 110%	Vitamin C 2% Calcium 4%	Iron 2%

PECAN PIE PROTEIN BARS

MAKES 12 PROTEIN BARS

128g (½ cup) **Roasted Pecan Butter**

1 cup **Unsweetened Vanilla Almond Milk**

1 teaspoon **English Toffee-Flavored Liquid Stevia Extract**

1½ cups **Graham Cracker Crumbs**

168g (1¼ cups, lightly packed) **Vanilla Brown Rice Protein Powder**

40g (⅓ cup) **Oat Flour**

1½ teaspoons **Ground Cinnamon**

¼ teaspoon **Salt**

1. Line an 8x8" brownie pan with parchment paper. Set aside.

2. In an electric stand mixer bowl fitted with a beater attachment, add all of the ingredients. Mix on low speed until everything is fully incorporated.

3. Scrape down the sides of the bowl. Mix on medium speed for one last mix. Mixture should be thick and fudgy, like cookie dough.

4. Scoop the mixture into the brownie pan and flatten it out. Tightly cover the pan with plastic wrap and refrigerate overnight.

5. Lift the mixture out of the pan. Slice into 12 bars. Individually wrap the protein bars in plastic sandwich baggies. Store in the refrigerator for up to 1 week or stash them in the freezer.

NUTRITION FACTS	Amount Per Serving		%Daily Value*
	Total Fat 9.5g	Total Carbohydrate 16.5g	
Serving Size 1 bar	Saturated Fat 0.5g	Dietary Fiber 4g	
Servings Per Recipe 12	Trans Fat 0g	Sugars 4g	
Calories 200	Cholesterol 0mg	Protein 13g	
Calories from Fat 90	Sodium 200mg		
*Percent Daily Value are based on a 2,000 calorie diet.	Vitamin A 0%	Vitamin C 0%	Calcium 8%	Iron 10%

TIRAMISÙ PROTEIN BARS

MAKES 12 PROTEIN BARS

PROTEIN BARS

128g (½ cup) **Raw Almond Butter**

¾ cup **Unsweetened Vanilla Almond Milk**

¼ cup **Brewed Espresso, cooled to room temperature**

1 teaspoon **Vanilla Crème-Flavored Liquid Stevia Extract**

168g (1¼ cups, lightly packed) **Vanilla Brown Rice Protein Powder**

80g (⅔ cup) **Oat Flour**

½ teaspoon **Espresso Powder**

¼ teaspoon **Salt**

MASCARPONE FROSTING

4oz **Mascarpone, room temperature**

½ tablespoon **Unsweetened Vanilla Almond Milk or Rum**

¼ teaspoon **Vanilla Crème-Flavored Liquid Stevia Extract**

2 tablespoons **Unsweetened Dutch Processed Cocoa Powder**

FOR THE PROTEIN BARS

1. Line an 8x8" brownie pan with parchment paper. Set aside.

2. In an electric stand mixer bowl fitted with a beater attachment, add all of the ingredients. Mix on low speed until everything is fully incorporated.

3. Scrape down the sides of the bowl. Mix on medium speed for one last mix. Mixture should be thick and fudgy, like cookie dough.

4. Scoop the mixture into the brownie pan and flatten it out.

FOR THE MASCARPONE FROSTING

5. In a medium-sized mixing bowl, whisk together the mascarpone, almond milk (or rum) and stevia extract. Scoop mixture over the protein bar base and spread to the edges of the pan (I used an offset spatula). Place in the freezer uncovered for 1 hour.

6. Lift the mixture out of the pan. Slice into 12 bars. Lightly dust the cocoa powder over the bars. To store, simply place a sheet of parchment paper on top of a cake pedestal, arrange the protein bars on top, and cover with a cake dome (keeps for ~5 days).

NUTRITION FACTS	Amount Per Serving		%Daily Value*
	Total Fat 10g	Total Carbohydrate 9g	
	Saturated Fat 3.5g	Dietary Fiber 3g	
Serving Size 1 bar	Trans Fat 0g	Sugars 1g	
Servings Per Recipe 12			
Calories 190	Cholesterol 10mg	Protein 14g	
Calories from Fat 90			
	Sodium 100mg		
*Percent Daily Value are based on a 2,000 calorie diet.	Vitamin A 0%	Vitamin C 0%	Calcium 8%	Iron 10%

FANCY PANTS FLAVORS

FANCY PANTS FLAVORS

NUTRITION FACTS

Serving Size 1 bar
Servings Per Recipe 12
Calories 270
   Calories from Fat 110

*Percent Daily Value are based
on a 2,000 calorie diet.

Amount Per Serving		%Daily Value*
Total Fat 12.5g	Total Carbohydrate 28g	
Saturated Fat 4g	Dietary Fiber 5g	
Trans Fat 0g	Sugars 16g	
Cholesterol 0mg	Protein 15g	
Sodium 160mg		

Vitamin A 0%	Vitamin C 0%	Calcium 10%	Iron 25%

S'MORES PROTEIN BARS

MAKES 12 PROTEIN BARS

PROTEIN BARS

128g (½ cup) **Roasted Almond Butter**

1 cup **Unsweetened Vanilla Almond Milk**

½ teaspoon **Vanilla Crème-Flavored Liquid Stevia Extract**

1⅓ cups **Graham Cracker Crumbs**

168g (1¼ cups, lightly packed) **Chocolate Brown Rice Protein Powder**

⅛ teaspoon **Salt**

TOPPINGS

6oz **Bittersweet Chocolate (70% cacao)**, melted

120 (~1½ cups/5oz) **All-Natural Mini Vanilla Marshmallows**

FOR PROTEIN BARS

1. Line an 8x8" brownie pan with parchment paper. Set aside.

2. In an electric stand mixer bowl fitted with a beater attachment, add all of the ingredients. Mix on low speed until everything is fully incorporated.

3. Scrape down the sides of the bowl. Mix on medium speed for one last mix. Mixture should be thick and fudgy, like cookie dough.

4. Scoop the mixture into the brownie pan and flatten it out. Tightly cover the pan with plastic wrap and refrigerate overnight.

5. Lift the mixture out of the pan. Slice into 12 bars.

FOR THE TOPPINGS

6. Place a silicone baking mat on top of a jelly roll pan and line the protein bars on top. With a large spoon, ladle the melted chocolate over the protein bars. Try to encase the entire protein bar with chocolate.

7. Press 10 mini marshmallows on top of each protein bar so they adhere as the chocolate firms up.

8. Refrigerate until firm (~1 hour). Individually wrap the protein bars in plastic sandwich baggies. Store in the refrigerator for up to 5 days or stash them in the freezer.

MO-TELLA PROTEIN BARS

What are MO-TELLA DIY Protein Bars you ask?
They taste like they're made with Nutella®, except they're healthy, wholesome, and all natural.
One bite and you'll be screaming, "Gimme mo of those MO-TELLA Protein Bars!"

MAKES 12 PROTEIN BARS

128g (½ cup) **Roasted Hazelnut Butter**

1 cup + 2 tablespoons **Unsweetened Vanilla Almond Milk**

1 teaspoon **Vanilla Crème-Flavored Liquid Stevia Extract**

168g (1¼ cups, lightly packed) **Chocolate Brown Rice Protein Powder**

80g (⅔ cup) **Oat Flour**

3 tablespoons **Unsweetened Dutch Processed Cocoa Powder**

¼ teaspoon **Salt**

¼ cup **No-Sugar-Added Chocolate Chips (or Mini Semi-Sweet Chocolate Chips)**

1. Line an 8x8" brownie pan with parchment paper. Set aside.

2. In an electric stand mixer bowl fitted with a beater attachment, add all of the ingredients. Mix on low speed until everything is fully incorporated.

3. Scrape down the sides of the bowl. Mix on medium speed for one last mix. Mixture should be thick and fudgy, like cookie dough.

4. Scoop the mixture into the brownie pan and flatten it out. Tightly cover the pan with plastic wrap and refrigerate overnight.

5. Lift the mixture out of the pan. Slice into 12 bars. Individually wrap the protein bars in plastic sandwich baggies. Store in the refrigerator for up to 1 week or stash them in the freezer.

NUTRITION FACTS	Amount Per Serving		%Daily Value*
	Total Fat 8g	**Total Carbohydrate** 10g	
Serving Size 1 bar	Saturated Fat 1.5g	Dietary Fiber 4g	
Servings Per Recipe 12	Trans Fat 0g	Sugars 2g	
Calories 160	**Cholesterol** 0mg	**Protein** 13g	
Calories from Fat 80			
*Percent Daily Value are based on a 2,000 calorie diet.	**Sodium** 95mg		
	Vitamin A 0% Vitamin C 0%	Calcium 10%	Iron 15%

Nutella® is a registered trademark of Ferro, SpA. Ferro, SpA is not related in any way to Desserts with Benefits, Inc.

MOCHA PROTEIN BARS

MAKES 10 PROTEIN BARS

128g (½ cup) **Roasted Almond Butter**

⅔ cup **Unsweetened Vanilla Almond Milk**

½ cup **Brewed Espresso, cooled to room temperature**

1¼ teaspoons **Vanilla Crème-Flavored Liquid Stevia Extract**

168g (1¼ cups, lightly packed) **Chocolate Brown Rice Protein Powder**

80g (⅔ cup) **Oat Flour**

2 tablespoons **Unsweetened Natural Cocoa Powder**

⅛ teaspoon **Salt**

¼ cup **No-Sugar-Added Chocolate Chips (or Mini Semi-Sweet Chocolate Chips)**

1. Line an 8x8" brownie pan with parchment paper. Set aside.

2. In an electric stand mixer bowl fitted with a beater attachment, add all of the ingredients. Mix on low speed until everything is fully incorporated.

3. Scrape down the sides of the bowl. Mix on medium speed for one last mix. Mixture should be thick and fudgy, like cookie dough.

4. Scoop the mixture into the brownie pan and flatten it out. Tightly cover the pan with plastic wrap and refrigerate overnight.

5. Lift the mixture out of the pan. Slice into 10 bars. Individually wrap the protein bars in plastic sandwich baggies. Store in the refrigerator for up to 1 week or stash them in the freezer.

NUTRITION FACTS	Amount Per Serving		%Daily Value*
	Total Fat 8g	Total Carbohydrate 12g	
Serving Size 1 bar	Saturated Fat 1.5g	Dietary Fiber 5g	
Servings Per Recipe 10	Trans Fat 0g	Sugars <1g	
Calories 190	Cholesterol 0mg	Protein 17g	
Calories from Fat 80	Sodium 75mg		
*Percent Daily Value are based on a 2,000 calorie diet.	Vitamin A 0% Vitamin C 0% Calcium 10%		Iron 20%

CARAMEL MACCHIATO PROTEIN BARS

MAKES 12 PROTEIN BARS

PROTEIN BARS

128g (½ cup) **Roasted Cashew Butter**

⅔ cup **Unsweetened Vanilla Almond Milk**

½ cup **Brewed Espresso, cooled to room temperature**

1 teaspoon **Vanilla Bean Paste**

1 teaspoon **English Toffee-Flavored Liquid Stevia Extract**

168g (1¼ cups, lightly packed) **Vanilla Brown Rice Protein Powder**

120g (1 cup) **Oat Flour**

¼ teaspoon **Salt**

CARAMEL-COFFEE FROSTING

⅓ cup **Organic Caramel Sauce** (see Pantry Staples on pg. ix)

75g (½ cup, packed) **Vanilla Brown Rice Protein Powder**

½ teaspoon **Espresso Powder**

FOR THE PROTEIN BARS

1. Line an 8x8" brownie pan with parchment paper. Set aside.

2. In an electric stand mixer bowl fitted with a beater attachment, add all of the ingredients. Mix on low speed until everything is fully incorporated.

3. Scrape down the sides of the bowl. Mix on medium speed for one last mix. Mixture should be thick and fudgy, like cookie dough.

4. Scoop the mixture into the brownie pan and flatten it out.

FOR THE CARAMEL-COFFEE FROSTING

5. In a small bowl, whisk together the caramel sauce, protein powder and espresso powder. Mixture should be like a thick, slightly sticky frosting. Spoon the mixture over the protein bar base and spread to the edges of the pan (I used an offset spatula). Place in the freezer uncovered for 1 hour.

6. Lift the mixture out of the pan. Slice into 12 bars. To store, simply place a sheet of parchment paper on top of a cake pedestal, arrange the protein bars on top, and cover with a cake dome (keeps for ~1 week).

NUTRITION FACTS

Serving Size 1 bar
Servings Per Recipe 12
Calories 200
  Calories from Fat 50

*Percent Daily Value are based
on a 2,000 calorie diet.

Amount Per Serving		%Daily Value*
Total Fat 6g	**Total Carbohydrate** 18g	
Saturated Fat 1.5g	**Dietary Fiber** 3g	
Trans Fat 0g	**Sugars** 6g	
Cholesterol 0mg	**Protein** 18g	
Sodium 115mg		
Vitamin A 0%	Vitamin C 0%	Calcium 4%	Iron 15%

NUTRITION FACTS

Serving Size 1 bar
Servings Per Recipe 12
Calories 240
   Calories from Fat 130

*Percent Daily Value are based on a 2,000 calorie diet.

Amount Per Serving		%Daily Value*
Total Fat 14g	**Total Carbohydrate** 14g	
Saturated Fat 4g	**Dietary Fiber** 5g	
Trans Fat 0g	**Sugars** 5g	
Cholesterol 0mg	**Protein** 15g	
Sodium 80mg		

Vitamin A 15%	Vitamin C 4%	Calcium 8%	Iron 20%

MINT CHOCOLATE PROTEIN BARS

MAKES 12 PROTEIN BARS

PROTEIN BARS

⅔ cup **Unsweetened Vanilla Almond Milk**

2½ cups **Baby Spinach, packed**

128g (½ cup) **Roasted Almond Butter**

2 teaspoons **Vanilla Crème-Flavored Liquid Stevia Extract**

2 teaspoons **Mint Flavor**

168g (1¼ cups, lightly packed) **Vanilla Brown Rice Protein Powder**

80g (⅔ cup) **Oat Flour**

⅛ teaspoon **Salt**

CHOCOLATE COATING

6oz **Bittersweet Chocolate (70% cacao), melted**

2 teaspoons **Mint Flavor**

FOR THE PROTEIN BARS

1. Line an 8x8" brownie pan with parchment paper. Set aside.

2. In a food processor, blend together the almond milk, spinach, almond butter, stevia extract, and mint flavor until completely smooth.

3. In an electric stand mixer bowl fitted with a beater attachment, add the green mixture, protein powder, oat flour, and salt. Mix on low speed until everything is fully incorporated.

4. Scrape down the sides of the bowl. Mix on medium speed for one last mix. Mixture should be thick and fudgy, like cookie dough.

5. Scoop the mixture into the brownie pan and flatten it out. Tightly cover the pan with plastic wrap and refrigerate overnight.

6. Lift the mixture out of the pan. Slice into 12 bars.

FOR THE CHOCOLATE COATING

7. Stir the mint flavor into the melted chocolate.

8. Place a silicone baking mat on top of a jelly roll pan and line the protein bars on top. With a large spoon, ladle the melted chocolate over the protein bars. Try to encase the entire protein bar with chocolate, but it doesn't have to be perfect.

9. Refrigerate until firm (~1 hour). Individually wrap the protein bars in plastic sandwich baggies. Store in the refrigerator for up to 4 days or stash them in the freezer.

MILLIONAIRE'S PROTEIN BARS

MAKES 12 PROTEIN BARS

PROTEIN BARS

128g (½ cup) **Roasted Almond Butter (Roasted Cashew Butter works great too!)**

1 cup + 2 tablespoons **Unsweetened Vanilla Almond Milk**

1 teaspoon **Vanilla Bean Paste**

1 teaspoon **Vanilla Crème-Flavored Liquid Stevia Extract**

90g (¾ cup) **Oat Flour**

84g (⅔ cup, packed) **Vanilla Brown Rice Protein Powder**

84g (⅔ cup, packed) **Chocolate Brown Rice Protein Powder** (you can swap the Chocolate with more Vanilla if you like)

¼ teaspoon **Flaked Sea Salt**

SALTED CARAMEL FROSTING

⅓ cup **Organic Caramel Sauce** (see Pantry Staples on pg. ix)

75g (½ cup, packed) **Vanilla Brown Rice Protein Powder**

⅛ teaspoon **Flaked Sea Salt**

CHOCOLATE COATING

6oz **Bittersweet Chocolate (70% cacao), melted**

FOR THE PROTEIN BARS

1. Line an 8x8" brownie pan with parchment paper. Set aside.

2. In an electric stand mixer bowl fitted with a beater attachment, add all of the ingredients. Mix on low speed until everything is fully incorporated.

3. Scrape down the sides of the bowl. Mix on medium speed for one last mix. Mixture should be thick and fudgy, like cookie dough.

4. Scoop the mixture into the brownie pan and flatten it out.

FOR THE SALTED CARAMEL FROSTING

5. In a small bowl, stir together the caramel sauce, protein powder and salt. Mixture should be thick and slightly sticky. Spoon the mixture over the protein bar base and spread to the edges of the pan. Place in the freezer uncovered for 1 hour.

6. Lift the mixture out of the pan. Slice into 12 bars.

FOR THE CHOCOLATE COATING

7 . Place a silicone baking mat on top of a jelly roll pan and line the protein bars on top. With a large spoon, ladle the melted chocolate over the protein bars. Try to encase the entire bar with chocolate. Feel free to top the bars with a sprinkle of flaked sea salt for decoration!

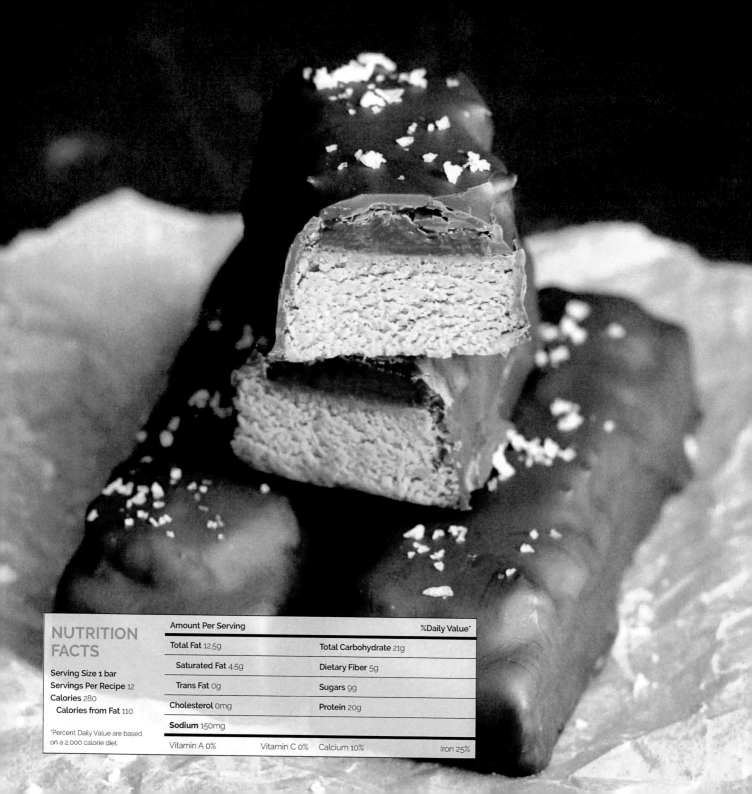

NUTRITION FACTS

Serving Size 1 bar
Servings Per Recipe 12
Calories 280
  Calories from Fat 110

*Percent Daily Value are based on a 2,000 calorie diet.

Amount Per Serving			%Daily Value*
Total Fat 12.5g		**Total Carbohydrate** 21g	
Saturated Fat 4.5g		**Dietary Fiber** 5g	
Trans Fat 0g		**Sugars** 9g	
Cholesterol 0mg		**Protein** 20g	
Sodium 150mg			
Vitamin A 0%	Vitamin C 0%	Calcium 10%	Iron 25%

SCOTCHEROOS PROTEIN BARS

MAKES 15 PROTEIN BARS

SCOTCHEROOS

120g (4 cups) **Crispy Brown Rice Cereal**

168g (½ cup) **Honey**

128g (½ cup) **Natural Peanut Butter**

1 teaspoon **Natural Butterscotch Flavor**

¼ teaspoon **Salt**

64g (⅔ cup) **Vanilla Whey Protein Powder**

CHOCOLATE TOPPING

3oz **Bittersweet Chocolate (70% cacao), melted**

FOR THE SCOTCHEROOS

1. Line an 8x8" brownie pan with parchment paper. Set aside.

2. In a medium-sized mixing bowl, add the crispy brown rice cereal.

3. In a large microwave-safe bowl, stir together the honey, peanut butter, butterscotch flavor and salt. Microwave at 10-second intervals, stirring between each one, until the mixture is runny and warm. Stir in the protein powder.

4. Fold in the crispy brown rice cereal. When everything is fully incorporated, scoop the mixture into the brownie pan and flatten it out with the silicone spatula. Be sure to press it down so you get a nice and compact cereal treat.

FOR THE CHOCOLATE TOPPING

5. Pour the melted chocolate over the base and tilt the pan around until the chocolate covers the entire surface. Tap the pan on the counter a few times to set the chocolate and get rid of any air bubbles. Refrigerate until firm (~1 hour).

6. Lift the mixture out of the pan. Slice into 15 bars (5 slices x 3 slices). Store in a tightly sealed container in the fridge with each treat placed on a square of parchment paper to prevent them from sticking (keeps for ~1 week).

NUTRITION FACTS	Amount Per Serving		%Daily Value*
	Total Fat 7g	Total Carbohydrate 20.5g	
Serving Size 1 bar	Saturated Fat 2g	Dietary Fiber 1g	
Servings Per Recipe 15	Trans Fat 0g	Sugars 10.5g	
Calories 170	Cholesterol <5mg	Protein 6g	
Calories from Fat 60	Sodium 90mg		
*Percent Daily Value are based on a 2,000 calorie diet.	Vitamin A 0% Vitamin C 0% Calcium 2%		Iron 4%

ELVIS PROTEIN BARS

MAKES 10 PROTEIN BARS

28g (½ cup) **Natural Peanut Butter**

1 cup **Unsweetened Vanilla Almond Milk**

1 teaspoon **Vanilla Crème-Flavored Liquid Stevia Extract**

1 teaspoon **Banana Flavor**

168g (1¼ cups, lightly packed) **Vanilla Brown Rice Protein Powder**

2oz (1¼ cups) **Freeze-Dried Bananas**

40g (⅓ cup) **Oat Flour**

¼ teaspoon **Salt**

1. Line an 8x8" brownie pan with parchment paper. Set aside.

2. In an electric stand mixer bowl fitted with a beater attachment, add all of the ingredients. Mix on low speed until everything is fully incorporated. Feel free to add ¼ cup of chopped peanuts!

3. Scrape down the sides of the bowl. Mix on medium speed for one last mix. Mixture should be thick and fudgy, like cookie dough, but with small chunks of banana throughout.

4. Scoop the mixture into the brownie pan and flatten it out. Tightly cover the pan with plastic wrap and refrigerate overnight.

5. Lift the mixture out of the pan. Slice into 10 bars. Individually wrap the protein bars in plastic sandwich baggies. Store in the refrigerator for up to 5 days or stash them in the freezer.

NUTRITION FACTS	Amount Per Serving		%Daily Value*
	Total Fat 7g	Total Carbohydrate 14g	
Serving Size **1 bar**	Saturated Fat 0.5g	Dietary Fiber 3g	
Servings Per Recipe 10	Trans Fat 0g	Sugars 5g	
Calories 180	Cholesterol 0mg	Protein 15g	
Calories from Fat 60	Sodium 120mg		
*Percent Daily Value are based on a 2,000 calorie diet.	Vitamin A 0% Vitamin C 0%	Calcium 6%	Iron 10%

PEANUT BUTTA & JELLY PROTEIN BARS

MAKES 12 PROTEIN BARS

2 cups **Unsweetened Vanilla Almond Milk**

128g (½ cup) **Natural Peanut Butter**

1 teaspoon **Vanilla Crème-Flavored Liquid Stevia Extract**

½ teaspoon **Strawberry Flavor**

210g (1¾ cups) **Peanut Flour**

168g (1¼ cups, lightly packed) **Vanilla Brown Rice Protein Powder**

½ cup **Quick-Cooking Oats**

¼ teaspoon **Salt**

2oz **Freeze-Dried Raspberries**

1. Line a 9x9" brownie pan with parchment paper. Set aside.

2. In an electric stand mixer bowl fitted with a beater attachment, add all of the ingredients except for the freeze-dried raspberries. Mix on low speed until everything is fully incorporated.

3. Scrape down the sides of the bowl. Add in the freeze-dried raspberries and mix on medium-low speed for one last mix. Mixture should be thick and fudgy, like cookie dough.

4. Scoop the mixture into the brownie pan and flatten it out. Tightly cover the pan with plastic wrap and refrigerate overnight.

5. Lift the mixture out of the pan. Slice into 12 bars. Individually wrap the protein bars in plastic sandwich baggies. Store in the refrigerator for up to 1 week or stash them in the freezer.

NUTRITION FACTS	Amount Per Serving		%Daily Value*
	Total Fat 8g	Total Carbohydrate 13g	
Serving Size 1 bar	Saturated Fat 1g	Dietary Fiber 6g	
Servings Per Recipe 12	Trans Fat 0g	Sugars 4g	
Calories 220	Cholesterol 0mg	Protein 23g	
Calories from Fat 70	Sodium 110mg		
*Percent Daily Value are based on a 2,000 calorie diet.	Vitamin A 0% Vitamin C 0%	Calcium 10%	Iron 10%

MATCHA GREEN TEA ALMOND PROTEIN BARS

MAKES 12 PROTEIN BARS

128g (½ cup) **Roasted Almond Butter**

1 cup + 2 tablespoons **Unsweetened Vanilla Almond Milk**

1½ teaspoons **Vanilla Crème-Flavored Liquid Stevia Extract**

¾ teaspoon **Almond Extract**

168g (1¼ cups, lightly packed) **Vanilla Brown Rice Protein Powder**

80g (⅔ cup) **Oat Flour**

2 tablespoons **Matcha Powder**

⅛ teaspoon **Salt**

1. Line an 8x8" brownie pan with parchment paper. Set aside.

2. In an electric stand mixer bowl fitted with a beater attachment, add all of the ingredients except. Mix on low speed until everything is fully incorporated.

3. Scrape down the sides of the bowl. Mix on medium speed for one last mix. Mixture should be thick and fudgy, like cookie dough.

4. Scoop the mixture into the brownie pan and flatten it out. Tightly cover the pan with plastic wrap and refrigerate overnight.

5. Lift the mixture out of the pan. Slice into 12 bars. Feel free to drizzle melted white, milk, or dark chocolate over the bars! Individually wrap the protein bars in plastic sandwich baggies. Store in the refrigerator for up to 1 week or stash them in the freezer.

NUTRITION FACTS	Amount Per Serving		%Daily Value*
Serving Size 1 bar **Servings Per Recipe** 12 **Calories** 150 Calories from Fat 50	**Total Fat** 6g	**Total Carbohydrate** 9g	
	Saturated Fat 0.5g	Dietary Fiber 3g	
	Trans Fat 0g	Sugars <1g	
	Cholesterol 0mg	Protein 14g	
	Sodium 75mg		
*Percent Daily Value are based on a 2,000 calorie diet.	Vitamin A 0%	Vitamin C 0% Calcium 6%	Iron 10%

SECRET GREENS PROTEIN BARS

MAKES 12 PROTEIN BARS

128g (½ cup) **Raw Almond Butter (Roasted Almond Butter works great too!)**

1 cup **Unsweetened Vanilla Almond Milk**

1½ teaspoons **Vanilla Crème-Flavored Liquid Stevia Extract**

1 teaspoon **Pure Vanilla Extract**

168g (1¼ cups, lightly packed) **Chocolate Brown Rice Protein Powder**

60g (½ cup) **Oat Flour**

50g (⅓ cup, packed) **Original Amazing Grass® Green Superfood® Powder**

¼ teaspoon **Salt**

¼ cup **Cacao Nibs (or Mini Semi-Sweet Chocolate Chips)**

1. Line an 8x8" brownie pan with parchment paper. Set aside.

2. In an electric stand mixer bowl fitted with a beater attachment, add all of the ingredients. Mix on low speed until everything is fully incorporated.

3. Scrape down the sides of the bowl. Mix on medium speed for one last mix. Mixture should be thick and fudgy, like cookie dough.

4. Scoop the mixture into the brownie pan and flatten it out. Tightly cover the pan with plastic wrap and refrigerate overnight.

5. Lift the mixture out of the pan. Slice into 12 bars. Individually wrap the protein bars in plastic sandwich baggies. Store in the refrigerator for up to 5 days or stash them in the freezer.

NUTRITION FACTS	Amount Per Serving	%Daily Value*
	Total Fat 8g	Total Carbohydrate 11g
Serving Size 1 bar	Saturated Fat 1.5g	Dietary Fiber 5g
Servings Per Recipe 12	Trans Fat 0g	Sugars <1g
Calories 180	Cholesterol 0mg	Protein 15g
Calories from Fat 70	Sodium 105mg	
*Percent Daily Value are based on a 2,000 calorie diet.	Vitamin A 15% Vitamin C 30% Calcium 15%	Iron 20%

CANDY BAR FLAVORS

CANDY BAR FLAVORS

PUMPED UP PROTEIN BARS

A Healthier Version of Milky Way®

MAKES 12 PROTEIN BARS

PROTEIN BARS

128g (½ cup) **Roasted Almond Butter**

1 cup + 2 tablespoons **Unsweetened Vanilla Almond Milk**

1 teaspoon **Vanilla Crème-Flavored Liquid Stevia Extract**

168g (1¼ cups, lightly packed) **Chocolate Brown Rice Protein Powder**

80g (⅔ cup) **Oat Flour**

¼ teaspoon **Salt**

CARAMEL LAYER

⅓ cup **Organic Caramel Sauce**
(see Pantry Staples on pg. ix)

63g (½ cup, lightly packed) **Vanilla Brown Rice Protein Powder**

CHOCOLATE-ALMOND COATING

6oz **Milk Chocolate with Salted Almonds, melted**

1 tablespoon **Coconut Oil, melted**

FOR THE PROTEIN BARS

1. Line an 8x8" brownie pan with parchment paper. Set aside.

2. In an electric stand mixer bowl fitted with a beater attachment, add all of the ingredients. Mix on low speed until everything is fully incorporated.

3. Scrape down the sides of the bowl. Mix on medium speed for one last mix. Mixture should be thick and fudgy, like cookie dough.

4. Scoop the mixture into the brownie pan and flatten it out.

FOR THE CARAMEL LAYER

5. In a small bowl, stir together the caramel sauce and protein powder. Mixture should be thick and slightly sticky. Spoon the mixture over the protein bar base and spread to the edges of the pan. Place in the freezer uncovered for 1 hour.

6. Lift the mixture out of the pan. Slice into 12 bars.

FOR THE CHOCOLATE-ALMOND COATING

7. Stir the coconut oil into the melted chocolate.

8. Place a silicone baking mat on top of a jelly roll pan and line the protein bars on top. With a large spoon, ladle the melted chocolate over the protein bars. Try to encase the entire bar with chocolate.

9. Refrigerate until firm (~1 hour). Individually wrap the protein bars in plastic sandwich baggies. Store in the refrigerator for up to 1 week or stash them in the freezer.

NUTRITION FACTS	Amount Per Serving		%Daily Value*
Serving Size 1 bar	Total Fat 13g	Total Carbohydrate 20g	
Servings Per Recipe 12	Saturated Fat 5g	Dietary Fiber 4g	
Calories 270	Trans Fat 0g	Sugars 11g	
Calories from Fat 120	Cholesterol 0mg	Protein 19g	
*Percent Daily Value are based on a 2,000 calorie diet.	Sodium 140mg		
	Vitamin A 0% Vitamin C 0% Calcium 15%		Iron 20%

FUN PROTEIN FACT

Peanut butter, almond butter, oats, garbanzo beans!

They are all high in protein, but they are incomplete proteins. This means that they don't contain all the essential amino acids necessary for muscle growth, repair and maintenance. These foods need to be paired with complementary proteins – proteins that contain those missing amino acids. For example, in these Pumped Up Protein Bars, you get a complete protein because the almond butter and oat flour "complement" each other. Together, they contain the essential amino acids you need!

Milky Way® is a registered trademark of Mars, Inc.   Mars, Inc. is not related in any way to Desserts with Benefits, Inc.

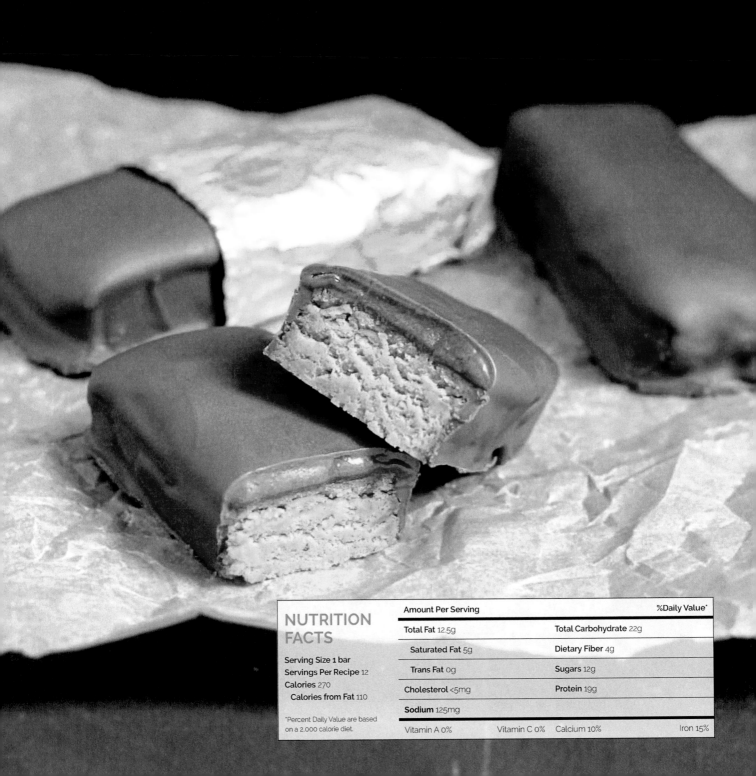

NUTRITION FACTS

Serving Size 1 bar
Servings Per Recipe 12
Calories 270
  Calories from Fat 110

*Percent Daily Value are based on a 2,000 calorie diet.

Amount Per Serving		%Daily Value*
Total Fat 12.5g	Total Carbohydrate 22g	
Saturated Fat 5g	Dietary Fiber 4g	
Trans Fat 0g	Sugars 12g	
Cholesterol <5mg	Protein 19g	
Sodium 125mg		
Vitamin A 0%	Vitamin C 0%	Calcium 10%	Iron 15%

SHREDDED PROTEIN BARS

A Healthier Version of Twix®

MAKES 12 PROTEIN BARS

PROTEIN BARS

128g (½ cup) **Roasted Almond Butter**

1 cup **Unsweetened Vanilla Almond Milk**

1 teaspoon **Vanilla Crème-Flavored Liquid Stevia Extract**

½ teaspoon **Natural Butter Flavor**

168g (1¼ cups, lightly packed) **Vanilla Brown Rice Protein Powder**

80g (⅔ cup) **Oat Flour**

¼ teaspoon **Salt**

CARAMEL LAYER

⅓ cup **Organic Caramel Sauce** (see Pantry Staples on pg. ix)

63g (½ cup, lightly packed) **Vanilla Brown Rice Protein Powder**

CHOCOLATE COATING

6oz **Milk Chocolate (34% cacao), melted**

1 tablespoon **Coconut Oil, melted**

FOR THE PROTEIN BARS

1. Line an 8x8" brownie pan with parchment paper. Set aside.

2. In an electric stand mixer bowl fitted with a beater attachment, add all of the ingredients. Mix on low speed until everything is fully incorporated.

3. Scrape down the sides of the bowl. Mix on medium speed for one last mix. Mixture should be thick and fudgy, like cookie dough.

4. Scoop the mixture into the brownie pan and flatten it out.

FOR THE CARAMEL LAYER

5. In a small bowl, stir together the caramel sauce and protein powder. Mixture should be thick and slightly sticky. Spoon the mixture over the protein bar base and spread to the edges of the pan (I used an offset spatula). Place in the freezer uncovered for 1 hour.

6. Lift the mixture out of the pan. Slice into 12 bars.

FOR THE CHOCOLATE COATING

7. Stir the coconut oil into the melted chocolate.

8. Place a silicone baking mat on top of a jelly roll pan and line the protein bars on top. With a large spoon, ladle the melted chocolate over the protein bars. Try to encase the entire bar with chocolate.

9. Refrigerate until firm (~1 hour). Individually wrap the protein bars in plastic sandwich baggies. Store in the refrigerator for up to 1 week or stash them in the freezer.

Twix® is a registered trademark of Mars, Inc. Mars, Inc. is not related in any way to Desserts with Benefits, Inc.

BEEFCAKE PROTEIN BARS

A Healthier Version of Snickers®

MAKES 12 PROTEIN BARS

PROTEIN BARS

128g (½ cup) **Natural Peanut Butter**

1 cup + 2 tablespoons **Unsweetened Vanilla Almond Milk**

1 teaspoon **Vanilla Crème-Flavored Liquid Stevia Extract**

168g (1¼ cups, lightly packed) **Vanilla Brown Rice Protein Powder**

80g (⅔ cup) **Oat Flour**

¼ teaspoon **Salt**

CARAMEL LAYER

⅓ cup **Organic Caramel Sauce** (see Pantry Staples on pg. ix)

63g (½ cup, lightly packed) **Vanilla Brown Rice Protein Powder**

¼ cup **Peanuts**

CHOCOLATE COATING

6oz **Milk Chocolate (34% cacao), melted**

1 tablespoon **Coconut Oil, melted**

FOR THE PROTEIN BARS

1. Line an 8x8" brownie pan with parchment paper. Set aside.

2. In an electric stand mixer bowl fitted with a beater attachment, add all of the ingredients. Mix on low speed until everything is fully incorporated.

3. Scrape down the sides of the bowl. Mix on medium speed for one last mix. Mixture should be thick and fudgy, like cookie dough.

4. Scoop the mixture into the brownie pan and flatten it out.

FOR THE CARAMEL LAYER

5. In a small bowl, stir together the caramel sauce and protein powder. Mixture should be thick and slightly sticky. Spoon the mixture over the protein bar base and spread to the edges of the pan. Sprinkle the chopped peanuts on top and press them into the surface. Place in the freezer uncovered for 1 hour.

6. Lift the mixture out of the pan. Slice into 12 bars.

FOR THE CHOCOLATE COATING

7. Stir the coconut oil into the melted chocolate.

8. Place a silicone baking mat on top of a jelly roll pan and line the protein bars on top. With a large spoon, ladle the melted chocolate over the protein bars. Try to encase the entire bar with chocolate.

9. Refrigerate until firm (~1 hour). Individually wrap the protein bars in plastic sandwich baggies. Store in the refrigerator for up to 1 week or stash them in the freezer.

Snickers® is a registered trademark of Mars, Inc. Mars, Inc. is not related in any way to Desserts with Benefits, Inc.

NUTRITION FACTS

Serving Size **1 bar**
Servings Per Recipe 12
Calories 290
  Calories from Fat 120

*Percent Daily Value are based on a 2,000 calorie diet.

Amount Per Serving		%Daily Value*
Total Fat 13g	**Total Carbohydrate** 23g	
Saturated Fat 5g	**Dietary Fiber** 4g	
Trans Fat 0g	**Sugars** 13g	
Cholesterol <5mg	**Protein** 19g	
Sodium 130mg		
Vitamin A 0%	Vitamin C 0% Calcium 8%	Iron 15%

Reese's® is a registered trademark of The Hershey Company. The Hershey Company is not related in any way to Desserts with Benefits, Inc.

IN THE BUFF PROTEIN BARS

A Healthier Version of Reese's®

MAKES 12 PROTEIN BARS

PROTEIN BARS

128g (½ cup) **Natural Peanut Butter**

1 cup + 2 tablespoons **Unsweetened Vanilla Almond Milk**

1 teaspoon **Vanilla Crème-Flavored Liquid Stevia Extract**

168g (1¼ cups, lightly packed) **Vanilla Brown Rice Protein Powder**

90g (¾ cup) **Peanut Flour**

¼ teaspoon **Salt**

CHOCOLATE COATING

6oz **Milk Chocolate (34% cacao), melted**

1 tablespoon **Coconut Oil, melted**

FOR THE PROTEIN BARS

1. Line an 8x8" brownie pan with parchment paper. Set aside.

2. In an electric stand mixer bowl fitted with a beater attachment, add all of the ingredients.

3. Scrape down the sides of the bowl. Mix on medium speed for one last mix. Mixture should be thick and fudgy, like cookie dough.

4. Scoop the mixture into the brownie pan and flatten it out. Tightly cover the pan with plastic wrap and refrigerate overnight.

5. Lift the mixture out of the pan. Slice into 12 bars.

FOR THE CHOCOLATE COATING

6. Stir the coconut oil into the melted milk chocolate.

7. Place a silicone baking mat on top of a jelly roll pan and line the protein bars on top. With a large spoon, ladle the melted chocolate over the protein bars. Try to encase the entire bar with chocolate, but it doesn't have to be perfect.

8. Refrigerate until firm (~1 hour). Individually wrap the protein bars in plastic sandwich baggies. Store in the refrigerator for up to 1 week or stash them in the freezer.

NUTRITION FACTS	Amount Per Serving		%Daily Value*
	Total Fat 12g	Total Carbohydrate 14g	
Serving Size 1 bar	Saturated Fat 4.5g	Dietary Fiber 3g	
Servings Per Recipe 12	Trans Fat 0g	Sugars 9g	
Calories 230	Cholesterol <5mg	Protein 18g	
Calories from Fat 110	Sodium 110mg		
*Percent Daily Value are based on a 2,000 calorie diet.	Vitamin A 0% Vitamin C 0%	Calcium 8%	Iron 10%

90

LET'S RACE PROTEIN BARS

A Healthier Version of Take5®

MAKES 12 PROTEIN BARS

PROTEIN BARS

128g (½ cup) **Natural Peanut Butter**

1 cup + 3 tablespoons **Unsweetened Vanilla Almond Milk**

1 teaspoon **Vanilla Crème-Flavored Liquid Stevia Extract**

168g (1¼ cups, lightly packed) **Vanilla Brown Rice Protein Powder**

90g (¾ cup) **Peanut Flour**

¼ teaspoon **Salt**

TOPPINGS

⅓ cup **Organic Caramel Sauce** (see Pantry Staples on pg. ix)

40g (⅓ cup) **Peanut Flour**

24 **Pretzel Rods**

¼ cup **Peanuts**

CHOCOLATE COATING

6oz **Bittersweet Chocolate (70% cacao), melted**

FOR THE PROTEIN BARS

1. Line an 8x8" brownie pan with parchment paper. Set aside.

2. In an electric stand mixer bowl fitted with a beater attachment, add all of the ingredients. Mix on low speed until everything is fully incorporated.

3. Scrape down the sides of the bowl. Mix on medium speed for one last mix. Mixture should be thick and fudgy, like cookie dough.

4. Scoop the mixture into the brownie pan and flatten it out.

FOR THE TOPPINGS

5. In a small bowl, stir together the caramel sauce and peanut flour. Mixture should be thick and slightly sticky. Spoon the mixture over the protein bar base and spread to the edges of the pan. Place in the freezer uncovered for 2 hours.

6. Lift the mixture out of the pan. Slice into 12 bars.

7. Press the pretzel rods (2 rods per bar) and peanuts into the caramel.

FOR THE CHOCOLATE COATING

8. Place a silicone baking mat on top of a jelly roll pan and line the protein bars on top. With a large spoon, ladle the melted chocolate over the protein bars. Try to encase the entire bar with chocolate.

9. Refrigerate until firm (~2 hours). Individually wrap the protein bars in plastic sandwich baggies. Store in the refrigerator (keeps for ~1 week, but the pretzels will be at their crunchiest for the first couple of days).

Take5® is a registered trademark of The Hershey Company. The Hershey Company is not related in any way to Desserts with Benefits, Inc.

NUTRITION FACTS

Serving Size 1 bar
Servings Per Recipe 12
Calories 320
   Calories from Fat 140

*Percent Daily Value are based on a 2,000 calorie diet.

Amount Per Serving		%Daily Value*
Total Fat 15g	**Total Carbohydrate** 25g	
Saturated Fat 5g	Dietary Fiber 6g	
Trans Fat 0g	Sugars 10g	
Cholesterol 0mg	Protein 21g	
Sodium 220mg		
Vitamin A 0%	Vitamin C 0%	Calcium 8%	Iron 20%

CHUBBY HUBBY PROTEIN BARS

MAKES 12 PROTEIN BARS

PROTEIN BARS

128g (½ cup) **Natural Peanut Butter**

1 cup + 3 tablespoons **Unsweetened Vanilla Almond Milk**

1 teaspoon **Vanilla Crème-Flavored Liquid Stevia Extract**

168g (1¼ cups, lightly packed) **Vanilla Brown Rice Protein Powder**

90g (¾ cup) **Peanut Flour**

¼ teaspoon **Salt**

TOPPINGS

3oz **Bittersweet Chocolate (70% cacao), melted**

36 **Pretzel Rods**

FOR THE PROTEIN BARS

1. Line an 8x8" brownie pan with parchment paper. Set aside.

2. In an electric stand mixer bowl fitted with a beater attachment, add all of the ingredients. Mix on low speed until everything is fully incorporated.

3. Scrape down the sides of the bowl. Mix on medium speed for one last mix. Mixture should be thick and fudgy, like cookie dough.

4. Scoop the mixture into the brownie pan and flatten it out. Tightly cover the pan with plastic wrap and refrigerate overnight.

5. Lift the mixture out of the pan. Slice into 12 bars.

FOR THE TOPPINGS

6. Place a silicone baking mat on top of a jelly roll pan and line the protein bars on top. Spread a little melted chocolate over a protein bar and press on 3 pretzel rods so they adhere to the chocolate. Do this with the rest of the protein bars. Drizzle the remaining chocolate over the protein bars.

7. Refrigerate until firm (~1 hour). Individually wrap the protein bars in plastic sandwich baggies. Store in the refrigerator for up to 1 week or stash them in the freezer.

NUTRITION FACTS	Amount Per Serving		%Daily Value*
	Total Fat 10.5g	Total Carbohydrate 21g	
Serving Size 1 bar	Saturated Fat 2.5g	Dietary Fiber 5g	
Servings Per Recipe 12	Trans Fat 0g	Sugars 4g	
Calories 250	Cholesterol 0mg	Protein 18g	
Calories from Fat 90	Sodium 270mg		
*Percent Daily Value are based on a 2,000 calorie diet.	Vitamin A 0% Vitamin C 0% Calcium 6%		Iron 15%

POWERHOUSE PROTEIN BARS

A Healthier Version of Payday®

MAKES 24 PROTEIN BARS

½ cup **Organic Caramel Sauce**
(see Pantry Staples on pg. ix)

128g (½ cup) **Natural Peanut Butter**

1 cup **Unsweetened Vanilla Almond Milk**

2 teaspoons **Vanilla Crème-Flavored Liquid Stevia Extract**

360g (3 cups) **Peanut Flour**

¼ teaspoon **Salt**

1 cup **Peanuts**

1. Line an 8x8" brownie pan with parchment paper. Set aside.

2. In an electric stand mixer bowl fitted with a beater attachment, add the caramel sauce, peanut butter, almond milk and stevia extract. Mix on low speed while you prepare the dry ingredients.

3. In a medium-sized mixing bowl, add the protein powder and salt. Turn off the stand mixer and dump in the dry ingredients. Return mixer to low speed and mix until the dry ingredients are fully incorporated. Scrape down the sides of the bowl. Mix on medium speed for one last mix.

4. Scoop the mixture into the brownie pan and flatten it out. Tightly cover the pan with plastic wrap and refrigerate overnight.

5. Lift the mixture out of the pan. Slice into 12 bars, then slice each bar in half lengthwise so you get 24 strips.

6. Press the peanuts into the strips. Individually wrap the protein bars in plastic sandwich baggies. Store in the refrigerator for up to 1 week or stash them in the freezer.

NUTRITION FACTS	Amount Per Serving		%Daily Value*
	Total Fat 7g	Total Carbohydrate 7g	
	Saturated Fat 1g	Dietary Fiber 3g	
Serving Size 1 bar	Trans Fat 0g	Sugars 5g	
Servings Per Recipe 24			
Calories 130	Cholesterol 0mg	Protein 10g	
Calories from Fat 60			
	Sodium 40mg		
*Percent Daily Value are based on a 2,000 calorie diet.	Vitamin A 2%	Vitamin C 0% Calcium 4%	Iron 6%

PayDay® is a registered trademark of The Hershey Company. The Hershey Company is not related in any way to Desserts with Benefits, Inc.

DYNAMIC PROTEIN BARS

A Healthier Version of Mounds®

MAKES 12 PROTEIN BARS

PROTEIN BARS

128g (½ cup) **Raw Coconut Butter, melted**

1 cup + 2 tablespoons **Unsweetened Vanilla Coconut Milk, room temperature**

1 teaspoon **Coconut-Flavored Liquid Stevia Extract**

168g (1¼ cups, lightly packed) **Vanilla Brown Rice Protein Powder**

36g (¼ cup) **Coconut Flour**

⅛ teaspoon **Salt**

CHOCOLATE-COCONUT COATING

6oz **Bittersweet Chocolate (70% cacao), melted**

64g (¼ cup) **Raw Coconut Butter**

FOR THE PROTEIN BARS

1. Line an 8x8" brownie pan with parchment paper. Set aside.

2. In an electric stand mixer bowl fitted with a beater attachment, add all of the ingredients. Mix on low speed until everything is fully incorporated.

3. Scrape down the sides of the bowl. Mix on medium speed for one last mix. Mixture should be thick and fudgy, like cookie dough.

4. Scoop the mixture into the brownie pan and flatten it out. Cover the pan with plastic wrap and refrigerate overnight.

5. Lift the mixture out of the pan and let it sit on the counter for 10 minutes to soften. Slice into 12 bars.

FOR THE CHOCOLATE-COCONUT COATING

6. Stir the coconut butter into the melted chocolate. Place a silicone baking mat on top of a jelly roll pan and line the protein bars on top. With a large spoon, ladle the melted chocolate over the protein bars. Try to encase the entire bar with chocolate, but it doesn't have to be perfect.

7. Refrigerate until firm (~1 hour). Individually wrap the protein bars in plastic sandwich baggies. Store in the refrigerator for up to 1 week or stash them in the freezer.

NUTRITION FACTS	Amount Per Serving		%Daily Value*
Serving Size 1 bar	Total Fat 16g	Total Carbohydrate 13g	
Servings Per Recipe 12	Saturated Fat 12g	Dietary Fiber 6g	
Calories 250	Trans Fat 0g	Sugars 5g	
Calories from Fat 140	Cholesterol 0mg	Protein 13g	
*Percent Daily Value are based on a 2,000 calorie diet.	Sodium 75mg		
	Vitamin A 0% Vitamin C 0% Calcium 6%		Iron 15%

Mounds® is a registered trademark of The Hershey Company. The Hershey Company is not related in any way to Desserts with Benefits, Inc.

DUO PROTEIN BARS

A Healthier Version of Almond Joy®

MAKES 12 PROTEIN BARS

PROTEIN BARS

128g (½ cup) **Raw Coconut Butter, melted**

1 cup + 2 tablespoons **Unsweetened Vanilla Coconut Milk, room temperature**

1 teaspoon **Coconut-Flavored Liquid Stevia Extract**

1 teaspoon **Almond Extract**

168g (1¼ cups, lightly packed) **Vanilla Brown Rice Protein Powder**

36g (¼ cup) **Coconut Flour**

⅛ teaspoon **Salt**

48 **Whole Almonds**

CHOCOLATE-COCONUT COATING

6oz **Bittersweet Chocolate (70% cacao), melted**

64g (¼ cup) **Raw Coconut Butter**

FOR THE PROTEIN BARS

1. Line an 8x8" brownie pan with parchment paper. Set aside.

2. In an electric stand mixer bowl fitted with a beater attachment, add the melted coconut butter, coconut milk, stevia extract and almond extract. Mix on low speed while you prepare the dry ingredients.

3. In a medium-sized mixing bowl, whisk together the protein powder, coconut flour and salt. Turn off the stand mixer and dump in the dry ingredients. Return mixer to low speed and mix until the dry ingredients are fully incorporated. Scrape down the sides of the bowl if necessary. Mixture should be thick and fudgy, like cookie dough.

4. Scoop the mixture into the brownie pan and flatten it out. Tightly cover the pan with plastic wrap and refrigerate overnight.

5. Lift the mixture out of the pan and let it sit on the counter for 10 minutes to soften. Slice into 12 bars. Press 4 almonds on top of each protein bar to make a line of almonds.

FOR THE CHOCOLATE-COCONUT COATING

6. Stir the coconut butter into the melted chocolate.

7. Place a silicone baking mat on top of a jelly roll pan and line the protein bars on top. With a large spoon, ladle the melted chocolate over the protein bars. Try to encase the entire bar with chocolate, but it doesn't have to be perfect.

8. Refrigerate until firm (~1 hour). Individually wrap the protein bars in plastic sandwich baggies. Store in the refrigerator for up to 1 week or stash them in the freezer.

Almond Joy® is a registered trademark of The Hershey Company. The Hershey Company is not related in any way to Desserts with Benefits, Inc.

NUTRITION FACTS

Serving Size 1 bar
Servings Per Recipe 12
Calories 270
   Calories from Fat 160

*Percent Daily Value are based on a 2,000 calorie diet.

Amount Per Serving		%Daily Value*
Total Fat 18g	Total Carbohydrate 13g	
Saturated Fat 12g	Dietary Fiber 7g	
Trans Fat 0g	Sugars 5g	
Cholesterol 0mg	Protein 14g	
Sodium 75mg		
Vitamin A 0% Vitamin C 0% Calcium 6%		Iron 15%

I'M SO RIPPED PROTEIN BARS

A Healthier Version of Cherry Ripe®

MAKES 12 PROTEIN BARS

PROTEIN BARS

128g (½ cup) **Raw Coconut Butter, melted**

1 cup + 2 tablespoons **Unsweetened Vanilla Coconut Milk, room temperature**

1 teaspoon **Coconut-Flavored Liquid Stevia Extract**

1 teaspoon **Cherry Flavor**

2 cups **Freeze-Dried Cherries, ground into a coarse powder** (measure after grinding)

168g (1¼ cups, lightly packed) **Vanilla Brown Rice Protein Powder**

⅛ teaspoon **Salt**

CHOCOLATE-COCONUT COATING

6oz **Bittersweet Chocolate (70% cacao), melted**

64g (¼ cup) **Raw Coconut Butter**

FOR THE PROTEIN BARS

1. Line an 8x8" brownie pan with parchment paper. Set aside.

2. In an electric stand mixer bowl fitted with a beater attachment, add all of the ingredients. Mix on low speed until everything is fully incorporated.

3. Scrape down the sides of the bowl. Mix on medium speed for one last mix. Mixture should be thick and fudgy, like cookie dough.

4. Scoop the mixture into the brownie pan and flatten it out. Cover the pan with plastic wrap and refrigerate overnight.

5. Lift the mixture out of the pan and let it sit on the counter for 10 minutes to soften. Slice into 12 bars.

FOR THE CHOCOLATE-COCONUT COATING

6. Stir the coconut butter into the melted chocolate. Place a silicone baking mat on top of a jelly roll pan and line the protein bars on top. With a large spoon, ladle the melted chocolate over the protein bars. Try to encase the entire bar with chocolate, but it doesn't have to be perfect.

7. Refrigerate until firm (~1 hour). Individually wrap the protein bars in plastic sandwich baggies. Store in the refrigerator for up to 1 week or stash them in the freezer.

NUTRITION FACTS	Amount Per Serving		%Daily Value*
	Total Fat 15g	Total Carbohydrate 27g	
Serving Size 1 bar	Saturated Fat 12g	Dietary Fiber 7g	
Servings Per Recipe 12	Trans Fat 0g	Sugars 19g	
Calories 300	Cholesterol 0mg	Protein 13g	
Calories from Fat 140	Sodium 70mg		
*Percent Daily Value are based on a 2,000 calorie diet.	Vitamin A 10%	Vitamin C 6%	Calcium 8%	Iron 20%

Cherry Ripe® is a registered trademark of Cadbury, Ltd. Cadbury, Ltd. is not related in any way to Desserts with Benefits, Inc.

THE ULTIMATE FLAVOR

A FLAVOR SO GOOD
IT NEEDS ITS
OWN SECTION!

DEATH BY CHOCOLATE PROTEIN BARS

(aka Quintuple Chocolate "Candy" Bars)

MAKES 12 PROTEIN BARS

PROTEIN BARS

128g (½ cup) **Roasted Almond Butter**

1 cup + 2 tablespoons **Unsweetened Vanilla Almond Milk**

1 teaspoon **Vanilla Crème-Flavored Liquid Stevia Extract**

½ teaspoon **Natural Butter Flavor**

168g (1¼ cups, lightly packed) **Chocolate Brown Rice Protein Powder**

80g (⅔ cup) **Oat Flour**

¼ cup **Unsweetened Natural Cocoa Powder**

¼ teaspoon **Salt**

CHOCOLATE FROSTING

230g (1 cup) **Plain, Nonfat Greek Yogurt**

½ teaspoon **Natural Butter Flavor**

½ teaspoon **Vanilla Crème-Flavored Liquid Stevia Extract**

2 tablespoons **Unsweetened Natural Cocoa Powder**

½ teaspoon **Psyllium Husk Powder**

¼ teaspoon **Espresso Powder**

CHOCOLATE COATING

6oz **Bittersweet Chocolate (70% cacao), melted**

¼ cup **Mini Semi-Sweet Chocolate Chips**

NOTE: You may substitute the yogurt and psyllium husk powder for cream cheese if you prefer!

FOR THE PROTEIN BARS

1. Line an 8x8" brownie pan with parchment paper. Set aside.

2. In an electric stand mixer bowl fitted with a beater attachment, add all of the ingredients. Mix on low speed until everything is fully incorporated.

3. Scrape down the sides of the bowl. Mix on medium speed for one last mix. Mixture should be thick and fudgy, like cookie dough.

4. Scoop the mixture into the brownie pan and flatten it out.

FOR THE CHOCOLATE FROSTING

5. In a medium-sized mixing bowl, whisk together the Greek yogurt, butter flavor, and stevia extract.

6. In a small bowl, whisk together the cocoa powder, psyllium husk powder and espresso powder. Dump the dry ingredients over the wet ingredients and whisk until smooth. Spoon the mixture over the protein bar base and spread to the edges of the pan (I used an offset spatula). Place in the freezer uncovered for 1 hour. Lift the mixture out of the pan. Slice into 12 bars.

FOR THE CHOCOLATE COATING

7. Place a silicone baking mat on top of a jelly roll pan and line the protein bars on top. With a large spoon, ladle the melted chocolate over the protein bars. Try to encase the entire bar with chocolate. Sprinkle the chocolate chips on top.

8. Refrigerate until firm (~1 hour). To store, simply place a sheet of parchment paper on top of a cake pedestal, arrange the protein bars on top, and cover with a cake dome (keeps for ~1 week).

NUTRITION FACTS	Amount Per Serving		%Daily Value*
Serving Size 1 bar **Servings Per Recipe** 12 **Calories** 240 **Calories from Fat** 120	Total Fat 13g	Total Carbohydrate 17g	
	Saturated Fat 5g	Dietary Fiber 6g	
	Trans Fat 0g	Sugars 8g	
	Cholesterol 0mg	Protein 18g	
*Percent Daily Value are based on a 2,000 calorie diet.	Sodium 100mg		
	Vitamin A 0% Vitamin C 0%	Calcium 15%	Iron 25%

Remember...

Food = Love

30851626R00077

Made in the USA
San Bernardino, CA